Federal Benefits for Veterans, Dependents and Survivors

2010 Edition

Department of Veterans Affairs

810 Vermont Ave., N.W.
Washington, DC 20420

U.S. GOVERNMENT OFFICIAL EDITION NOTICE

Use of ISBN

This is the official U.S. government edition of this publication and is herein identified to certify its authenticity. Use of the 0-16 ISBN prefix is for U.S. Government Printing Office Official Editions only. The Superintendent of Documents of the U.S. Government Printing Office requests that any reprinted edition clearly be labeled as a copy of the authentic work with a new ISBN.

Legal Status and Use of Seals and Logos

The seal of the Department of Veterans Affairs authenticates the 2010 edition of Federal Benefits for Veterans, Dependents and Survivors as the official summary of benefits that have been separately promulgated under Federal regulations established under Register Act. Under the provisions of 38 Code of Federal Regulations 1.9(f), it is prohibited to use the official seal, replicas, reproductions, or embossed seals of the Department of Veterans Affairs on any republication of this material without the express, written permission of the Secretary or Deputy Secretary of Veterans Affairs. Any person using official seals and logos of the Department of Veterans Affairs in a manner inconsistent with the provisions of 38 Code of Federal Regulations 1.9 may be subject to the penalties specified in 18 United States Code 506, 701, or 1017 as applicable.

For sale by the Superintendent of Documents, U.S. Government Printing Office
Internet: bookstore.gpo.gov Phone: toll free (866) 512-1800; DC area (202) 512-1800
Fax: (202) 512-2104 Mail: Stop IDCC, Washington, DC 20401

ISBN 978-0-16-085220-6

Contents

Introduction

Veterans of the United States armed forces may be eligible for a broad range of programs and services provided by the U.S. Department of Veterans Affairs (VA). These benefits are legislated in Title 38 of the United States Code. This booklet contains a summary of these benefits effective Jan. 1, 2010. For additional information, visit the VA Web page at www.va.gov/.

La versión en español de este folleto se encuentra disponible en formato Adobe Acrobat a través de el link: www1.va.gov/opa/feature/index.asp.

General Eligibility

Eligibility for most VA benefits is based upon discharge from active military service under other than dishonorable conditions. Active service means full-time service, other than active duty for training, as a member of the Army, Navy, Air Force, Marine Corps, Coast Guard, or as a commissioned officer of the Public Health Service, Environmental Science Services Administration or National Oceanic and Atmospheric Administration, or its predecessor, the Coast and Geodetic Survey. Generally, men and women veterans with similar service may be entitled to the same VA benefits.

Dishonorable and bad conduct discharges issued by general courts-martial may bar VA benefits. Veterans in prison and parolees must contact a VA regional office to determine eligibility. VA benefits will not be provided to any veteran or dependent wanted for an outstanding felony warrant.

Certain VA Benefits Require Wartime Service

Certain VA benefits require service during wartime. Under the law, VA recognizes these war periods:

Mexican Border Period: May 9, 1916, through April 5, 1917, for veterans who served in Mexico, on its borders or in adjacent waters.

World War I: April 6, 1917, through Nov. 11, 1918; for veterans who served in Russia, April 6, 1917, through April 1, 1920; extended through July 1, 1921, for veterans who had at least one day of service between April 6, 1917, and Nov. 11, 1918.

World War II: Dec. 7, 1941, through Dec. 31, 1946.

Korean War: June 27, 1950, through Jan. 31, 1955.

Vietnam War: Aug. 5, 1964 (Feb. 28, 1961, for veterans who served "in country" before Aug. 5, 1964), through May 7, 1975.

Gulf War: Aug. 2, 1990, through a date to be set by law or Presidential Proclamation.

Important Documents Needed to Expedite

VA Benefits Delivery

In order to expedite benefits delivery, veterans seeking a VA benefit for the first time must submit a copy of their service discharge form (DD-214, DD-215, or for World War II veterans, a WD form), which documents service dates and type of discharge, or give their full name, military service number, and branch and dates of service. The veteran's service discharge form should be kept in a safe location accessible to the veteran and next of kin or designated representative.

The following documents will be needed for claims processing related to a veteran's death:

1. Veteran's marriage certificate for claims of a surviving spouse or children.

2. Veteran's death certificate if the veteran did not die in a VA health care facility.

3. Children's birth certificates or adoption papers to determine children's benefits.

4. Veteran's birth certificate to determine parents' benefits.

Abbreviations

ALS – Amyotrophic Lateral Sclerosis
CHAMPVA – Civilian Health and Medical Program of VA
CLC – Community Living Center
C&P – Compensation and Pension
COE – Certificate of Eligibility
CRDP – Concurrent Retirement and Disability Payments
CRSC – Combat-Related Special Compensation
CWT – Compensated Work Therapy
CZTE – Combat Zone Tax Exclusion
DIC – Dependency and Indemnity Compensation
DoD -- Department of Defense
FHA – Federal Housing Administration
FSGLI – Family Servicemembers' Group Life Insurance
HUD – Department of Housing and Urban Development
IRR – Individual Ready Reserve
MGIB – Montgomery GI Bill
MIA – Missing in Action
NPRC – National Personnel Records Center
NSLI – National Service Life Insurance
OEF – Operation Enduring Freedom
OIF – Operation Iraqi Freedom
OPM – Office of Personnel Management
POW -- Prisoner of War
PTSD – Post-Traumatic Stress Disorder
SAH – Specially Adapted Housing
SBA – Small Business Administration
SSI – Supplemental Security Income
S-DVI – Service-Disabled Veterans' Insurance
SGLI – Servicemembers' Group Life Insurance
SSB – Special Separation Benefits
TAP – Transition Assistance Program
TSGLI – Servicemembers' Group Life Insurance Traumatic Injury Protection
USCIS – U.S. Citizenship and Immigration Services
USDA – U.S. Department of Agriculture
VA – Department of Veterans Affairs
VEAP – Veterans Educational Assistance Program
VEOA – Veterans' Employment Opportunities Act
VGLI – Veterans' Group Life Insurance
VHA – Veterans Health Administration
VMET – Verification of Military Experience and Training
VMLI – Veterans' Mortgage Life Insurance
VR&E – Vocational Rehabilitation and Employment
VSI – Voluntary Separation Incentive
WAAC – Women's Army Auxiliary Corps
WASPs – Women Air Force Service Pilots

Chapter 1

VA Health Care Benefits

VA operates the nation's largest integrated health care system with more than 1,400 sites of care, including hospitals, community clinics, community living centers, domiciliary, readjustment counseling centers, and various other facilities. For additional information on VA health care, visit: www.va.gov/health.

Basic Eligibility

A person who served in the active military, naval, or air service and who was discharged or released under conditions other than dishonorable may qualify for VA health care benefits. Reservists and National Guard members may also qualify for VA health care benefits if they were called to active duty (other than for training only) by a Federal order and completed the full period for which they were called or ordered to active duty.

Minimum Duty Requirements: Veterans who enlisted after Sept. 7, 1980, or who entered active duty after Oct. 16, 1981, must have served 24 continuous months or the full period for which they were called to active duty in order to be eligible. This minimum duty requirement may not apply to veterans discharged for hardship, early out or a disability incurred or aggravated in the line of duty.

Enrollment

For most veterans, entry into the VA health care system begins by applying for enrollment. To apply, complete VA Form 10-10EZ, Application for Health Benefits, which may be obtained from any VA health care facility or regional benefits office, on line at www.va.gov/1010ez.htm or by calling 1-877-222-VETS (8387). Once enrolled, veterans can receive health care at VA health care facilities anywhere in the country.

Veterans enrolled in the VA health care system are afforded privacy rights under federal law. VA's Notice of Privacy Practices, which describes how VA may use and disclose veterans' medical information, is also available on line at www.va.gov/vhapublications/viewpublication.asp?pub_ID=1089

The following four categories of veterans are not required to enroll, but are urged to do so to permit better planning of health resources:
1. Veterans with a service-connected disability of 50 percent or more.
2. Veterans seeking care for a disability the military determined was incurred or aggravated in the line of duty, but which VA has not yet rated, within 12 months of discharge.
3. Veterans seeking care for a service-connected disability only.
4. Veterans seeking registry examinations (Ionizing Radiation, Agent Orange, Gulf War/Operation Iraqi Freedom and Depleted Uranium).

Priority Groups

During enrollment, each veteran is assigned to a priority group. VA uses priority groups to balance demand for VA health care enrollment with resources. Changes in available resources may reduce the number of priority groups VA can enroll. If this occurs, VA will publicize the changes and notify affected enrollees. A description of priority groups follows:

Group 1: Veterans with service-connected disabilities rated 50 percent or more and/or veterans determined by VA to be unemployable due to service-connected conditions.

Group 2: Veterans with service-connected disabilities rated 30 or 40 percent.

Group 3: Veterans with service-connected disabilities rated 10 and 20 percent; veterans who are former Prisoners of War (POW) or were awarded a Purple Heart medal; veterans awarded special eligibility for disabilities incurred in treatment or participation in a VA Vocational Rehabilitation program; and veterans whose discharge was for a disability incurred or aggravated in the line of duty.

Group 4: Veterans receiving aid and attendance or housebound benefits and/or veterans determined by VA to be catastrophically disabled.

Group 5: Veterans receiving VA pension benefits or eligible for Medicaid programs, and non service-connected veterans and non-compensable, zero percent service-connected veterans whose gross annual household income and/or net worth are below the VA national income threshold and geographically-adjusted income threshold for their resident area.

Group 6: Veterans of World War I; veterans seeking care solely for certain conditions associated with exposure to ionizing radiation during atmospheric testing or during the occupation of Hiroshima and Nagasaki; for any illness associated with participation in tests conducted by the Department of Defense (DoD) as part of Project 112/Project SHAD; veterans with zero percent service-connected disabilities who are receiving disability compensation benefits and veterans who served in a theater of combat operations after Nov. 11, 1998 as follows:

1. Veterans discharged from active duty on or after Jan. 28, 2003, who were enrolled as of Jan. 28, 2008 and veterans who apply for enrollment after Jan. 28, 2008, for 5 years post discharge
2. Veterans discharged from active duty before Jan. 28, 2003, who apply for enrollment after Jan. 28, 2008, until Jan. 27, 2011

Group 7: Veterans with gross household income below the geographically-adjusted income threshold (GMT) for their resident location and who agree to pay copays.

Group 8: Veterans with gross household income and/or net worth above the VA national income threshold and the geographic income threshold who agree to pay copays.
Note: Due to income relaxation rules implemented on June 15, 2009 Veterans with household income above the VA national threshold or the GMT income threshold for their resident location by 10 percent or less, who agree to pay copays, are eligible for enrollment in Priority Group 8.

The GMT thresholds can be located at: http://www.va.gov/healtheligibility/library/pubs/gmtincomethresholds.

Recently Discharged Combat Veterans
Veterans, including activated reservists and members of the National Guard, are eligible for the enhanced "Combat Veteran" benefits if they served on active duty in a theater of combat operations after November 11, 1998, and have been discharged under other than

dishonorable conditions.
Effective Jan. 28, 2008, combat veterans discharged from active duty on or after Jan. 28, 2003, are eligible for enhanced enrollment placement into Priority Group 6 (unless eligible for higher enrollment Priority Group placement) for five-years post discharge.

Veterans with combat service after Nov. 11, 1998, who were discharged from active duty before Jan. 28, 2003, and who apply for enrollment on or after Jan. 28, 2008, are eligible for this enhanced enrollment benefit through Jan. 27, 2011. During this period of enhanced enrollment benefits, these veterans receive VA care and medications at no cost for any condition that may be related to their combat service.

Veterans who enroll with VA under this "Combat Veteran" authority will retain enrollment eligibility even after their five-year post discharge period ends. At the end of their post discharge period, VA will reassess the Veteran's information (including all applicable eligibility factors) and make a new enrollment decision. For additional information, call 1-877-222-VETS (8387).

Special Access to Care
Service-Disabled Veterans: who are 50 percent or more disabled from service-connected conditions, unemployable due to service-connected conditions, or receiving care for a service-connected disability receive priority in scheduling of hospital or outpatient medical appointments.

Women Veterans
Women veterans are eligible for the same VA benefits as male veterans. Comprehensive health services are available to women veterans including primary care, specialty care, mental health care and reproductive health care services.

VA provides management of acute and chronic illnesses, preventive care, contraceptive services, menopause management, and cancer screenings, including pap smear and mammograms, and gynecology. Maternity care is covered in the Medical Benefits package and referrals are made to appropriate clinicians in the community for services that VA is unable to provide. Infertility evaluation and limited treatments are also available. For information, visit www.publichealth.

va.gov/womenshealth
Women Veterans Program Managers are available at all VA facilities. See the facility locator at www2.va.gov/directory/guide/home.
asp?isFlash=1 to help veterans seeking treatment and benefits. For
additional information, visit www.publichealth.va.gov/womenshealth/.

Sexual Trauma

VA health care professionals provide counseling and treatment to
help veterans overcome psychological issues resulting from sexual
trauma that occurred while serving on active duty, or active duty for
training if service was in the National Guard or Reserves. Veterans
who are not otherwise eligible for VA health care may still receive
these services. Appropriate services are provided for any injury,
illness or psychological condition resulting from such trauma. For additional information visit: www.ptsd.va.gov/public/index.asp

Financial Assessment

Most veterans not receiving VA disability compensation or pension
payments must provide information on their gross annual household
income and net worth to determine whether they are below the annually adjusted financial thresholds. Veterans who decline to disclose
their information or have income above the thresholds must agree
to pay copays in order to receive certain health benefits, effectively
placing them in Priority Group 8. VA is currently not enrolling new applicants who decline to provide financial information unless they have
a special eligibility factor.

This financial assessment includes all household income and net
worth, including Social Security, retirement pay, unemployment insurance, interest and dividends, workers' compensation, black lung benefits and any other income. Also considered are assets such as the
market value of property that is not the primary residence, stocks,
bonds, notes, individual retirement accounts, bank deposits, savings
accounts and cash.

VA also compares veterans' financial assessment with geographically based income thresholds. If the veteran's gross annual household
income is above VA's national means test threshold and below VA's
geographic means test threshold, or is below both the VA national
threshold and the VA geographically based threshold, but their
gross annual household income plus net worth exceeds VA's ceiling
(currently $80,000) the veteran may be eligible for Priority Group 7

placement and qualify for an 80-percent reduction in inpatient copay rates.

VA Medical Services and Medication Copays

Some veterans are required to make copays to receive VA health care and/or medications.

Inpatient Care: Priority Group 7 and certain other veterans are responsible for paying 20 percent of VA's inpatient copay or $213.60 for the first 90 days of inpatient hospital care during any 365-day period. For each additional 90 days, the charge is $106.80. In addition, there is a $2 per diem charge.

Priority Group 8 and certain other veterans are responsible for VA's inpatient copay of $1,100 for the first 90 days of care during any 365-day period. For each additional 90 days, the charge is $550. In addition, there is a $10 per diem charge.

Extended Care: For extended care services, veterans may be subject to a copay determined by information supplied by completing a VA Form 10-10EC. VA social workers can help veterans interpret their eligibility and copay requirements. The copay amount is based on each veteran's financial situation and is determined upon application for extended care services and will range from $0 to $97 a day.

Outpatient Care: A three-tiered copay system is used for all outpatient services. The copay is $15 for a primary care visit and $50 for some specialized care. Service-connected Veterans 10 percent or greater are exempt from copay requirements for inpatient and outpatient medical care for service-connected and non-service connected treatment. 0 percent service-connected Veterans may be required to complete a copay test to determine if copay requirements are advised.

Outpatient Visits Not Requiring Copays: Certain services are not charged a copay. Copays do not apply to publicly announced VA health fairs or outpatient visits solely for preventive screening and/ or vaccinations, such as vaccinations for influenza and pneumococcal, or screening for hypertension, hepatitis C, tobacco, alcohol, hyperlipidemia, breast cancer, cervical cancer, colorectal cancer by fecal occult blood testing, education about the risks and benefits of prostate cancer screening, HIV testing and counseling, and weight reduction or smoking cessation counseling (individual and group).

Laboratory, flat film radiology, electrocardiograms, and hospice care are also exempt from copays. While hepatitis C screening and HIV testing and counseling are exempt, medical care for HIV and hepatitis C are NOT exempt from copays.

Medication: Many non-service connected veterans are charged $8 for each 30-day or less supply of medication provided by VA for treatment of non-service connected conditions. For veterans enrolled in Priority Groups 2 through 6, the maximum copay for medications that will be charged in calendar year 2009 is $960 to 40 percent service-connected Veterans are responsible for paying a copay for non-service connected medications The following groups of veterans are not charged medication copays: veterans with a service-connected disability of 50 percent or more; veterans receiving medication for service-connected conditions; veterans whose annual income does not exceed the maximum annual rate of the VA pension; veterans enrolled in Priority Group 6 who receive medication under their special authority; veterans receiving medication for conditions related to sexual trauma related to service on active duty; certain veterans receiving medication for treatment of cancer of the head or neck; veterans receiving medication for a VA-approved research project; and former POWs.

NOTE: Copays apply to prescription and over-the-counter medications, such as aspirin, cough syrup or vitamins, dispensed by a VA pharmacy. However, veterans may prefer to purchase over-the-counter drugs, such as aspirin or vitamins, at a local pharmacy rather than making the copay. Copays are not charged for medications injected during the course of treatment or for medical supplies, such as syringes or alcohol wipes.

HSA/HRA: Health Savings Accounts (HSA) cannot be utilized to make VA copays. In addition, if the Veteran receives any health benefits from the VA or one of its facilities, including prescription drugs, in the last three months, he/she will not be eligible for an HSA. Health Reimbursement Arrangements (HRA) is not considered health plans and third party payers cannot be billed.

Private Health Insurance Billing
VA is required to bill private health insurance providers for medical care, supplies and prescriptions provided for treatment of veterans' non-service-connected conditions. Generally, VA cannot bill Medi-

care, but can bill Medicare supplemental health insurance for covered services. VA is not authorized to bill a High Deductible Health Plan (which is usually linked to a Health Savings Account).

All veterans applying for VA medical care are required to provide information on their health insurance coverage, including coverage provided under policies of their spouses. Veterans are not responsible for paying any remaining balance of VA's insurance claim not paid or covered by their health insurance, and any payment received by VA may be used to offset "dollar for dollar" a veteran's VA copay responsibility.

Reimbursement of Travel Costs

Certain veterans may be provided special mode travel (e.g. wheelchair van, ambulance) or reimbursed for travel costs when traveling for approved VA medical care. Reimbursement is paid at 41.5 cents per mile and is subject to a deductible of $3 for each one-way trip and $6 for a round trip; with a maximum deductible of $18 or the amount after six one-way trips (whichever occurs first) per calendar month. Two exceptions to the deductible are travel in relation to a VA compensation or pension examination and travel requiring a special mode of transportation. The deductible may be waived when their imposition would cause a severe financial hardship.

Eligibility: The following are eligible for VA travel:
1. Veterans whose service-connected disabilities are rated 30 percent or more.
2. Veterans traveling for treatment of service-connected conditions.
3. Veterans who receive a VA pension.
4. Veterans traveling for scheduled compensation or pension examinations.
5. Veterans whose gross household income does not exceed the maximum annual VA pension rate.
6. Veterans in certain emergency situations.
7. Veterans whose medical condition requires a special mode of transportation, if they are unable to defray the costs and travel is pre-authorized. Advance authorization is not required in an emergency if a delay would be hazardous to life or health.

8. Certain non-veterans when related to care of a veteran (attendants & donors).

Beneficiary travel fraud can take money out of the pockets of deserving Veterans. Inappropriate uses of beneficiary travel benefits include: incorrect addresses provided resulting in increase mileage; driving/riding together and making separate claims; and taking no cost transportation, such as DAV, and making claims. Veterans making false statements for beneficiary travel reimbursement may be prosecuted under applicable laws.

Reporting Fraud: Help VA's Secretary ensure integrity by reporting suspected fraud, waste or abuse in VA programs or operations.

VAOIG hotline: 1-800-488-8244
E-mail: vaoighotline@va.gov
Fax: (202) 565-7936

VA Inspector General Hotline
P.O. Box 50410
Washington, DC 20091-0410

VA Medical Programs

Veteran Health Registries

Certain veterans can participate in a VA health registry and receive free medical examinations, including laboratory and other diagnostic tests deemed necessary by an examining clinician. VA maintains health registries to provide special health examinations and health-related information. To participate, contact the Environmental Health (EH) Coordinator at the nearest VA health care facility or visit www.publichealth.va.gov/exposures, where a directory of EH Coordinators is maintained.

Gulf War Registry: For veterans who served on active military duty in Southwest Asia during the Gulf War, which began in 1990 and continues to the present, including Operation Iraqi Freedom (OIF). The Gulf War examination registry was established after the first Gulf War to identify possible diseases resulting from U.S. military personnel service in certain areas of Southwest Asia. These diseases were endemic to the area or may have been due to hazardous exposures, including heavy metals. Furthermore, air pollutants, i.e., carbon monoxide sulfur oxides, hydrocarbons, particulate matter, and nitrogen oxides, singly or in combination, could have caused chronic health problems.

Depleted Uranium Registries: Depleted uranium is natural uranium left over after most of the U-235 isotope has been removed, such as that used as fuel in nuclear power plants. DU possesses about 60 percent of the radioactivity of natural uranium; it is a radiation hazard primarily if internalized, such as in shrapnel, contaminated wounds, and inhalation. In addition to its radioactivity, DU has some chemical toxicity related to being a heavy metal (similar to lead).

Veterans who are identified by the Department of Defense (DoD) or have concerns about possible depleted uranium (DU) exposure are eligible for a DU evaluation. VA maintains two registries for veterans possibly exposed to depleted uranium. The first is for veterans who served in the Gulf War, including Operation Iraqi Freedom. The second is for veterans who served elsewhere, including Bosnia and Afghanistan.

Agent Orange Registry: For veterans possibly exposed to dioxin or other toxic substances in herbicides used during the Vietnam War, between 1962 and 1975, regardless of length of service, or while serving in Korea in 1968 or 1969, or as a result of testing, transporting, or spraying herbicides for military purposes. DoD has provided a list of locations and dates where herbicides, including Agent Orange, were used. This DoD list is available at www.publichealth.va.gov/exposures. For those sites not listed, the Vietnam Veteran should provide some proof of exposure to obtain a registry examination.

Ionizing Radiation Registry: For Veterans possibly exposed to and who are concerned about possible adverse effects of their atomic exposure during the following activities -- On-site participation in: an atmospheric detonation of a nuclear device, whether or not the testing nation was the United States; occupation of Hiroshima or Nagasaki from Aug. 6, 1945, through July 1, 1946; or internment as a POW in Japan during World War II, which the Secretary of Veterans Affairs determines resulted in an opportunity for exposure to ionizing radiation comparable to that of Veterans involved in the occupation of Hiroshima or Nagasaki.

In addition, VA regulations provide that "radiation-risk activity" means service at: Department of Energy gaseous diffusion plants at Paducah, Kentucky, Portsmouth, Ohio, or the K-25 area at Oak Ridge, Tennessee for at least 250 days before Feb. 1, 1992. If the Veteran was monitored for each of the 250 days using dosimetry badges to monitor radiation to external body parts or if the Veteran served for at least 250 days in a position that had exposures comparable to a job that was monitored using dosimetry badges; Longshot, Milrow or Cannikin underground nuclear tests at Amchitka Island, Alaska, before Jan. 1, 1974 or Veterans who received nasopharyngeal (NP) – nose and throat - radium irradiation treatments while in the active military, naval, or air service.

Readjustment Counseling Services

VA provides outreach and readjustment counseling services through 232 community-based Vet Centers located in all 50 states, the District of Columbia, Guam, Puerto Rico, American Samoa, and the U.S. Virgin Islands.

Eligibility: Veterans are eligible if they served on active duty in a combat theater during World War II, the Korean War, the Vietnam War, the Gulf War, or the campaigns in Lebanon, Grenada, Panama, Somalia, Bosnia, Kosovo, Afghanistan, Iraq and the Global War on Terror. Veterans, who served in the active military during the Vietnam-era, but not in the Republic of Vietnam, must have requested services at a Vet Center before Jan. 1, 2004. Vet Centers do not require enrollment in the VHA Health Care System.

Services Offered: Vet Center counselors provide individual, group, and family readjustment counseling to combat veterans to assist them in making a successful transition from military to civilian life; counseling services treatment for post-traumatic stress disorder (PTSD) and help with any other military related problems that affect functioning within the family, work, school or other areas of everyday life; other psycho-social services include outreach, education, medical referral, homeless veteran services, employment, VA benefit referral, and the brokering of non-VA services. The Vet Centers also provide military sexual trauma counseling to Veterans of both genders and of any era of military service.

Bereavement Counseling related to Servicemembers: Bereavement counseling is available through Department of Veterans Affairs (VA's) Vet Centers to all immediate family members (including spouses, children, parents, and siblings) of servicemembers who die in the line of duty while on active service. This includes federally-activated members of the National Guard and reserve components. Vet Center bereavement services for surviving family members of service members may be accessed by calling (202) 461-6530.

For additional information, contact the nearest Vet Center, listed in the back of this book, or visit www.vetcenter.va.gov/.

Prosthetic and Sensory Aids

Veterans receiving VA care for any condition may receive VA prosthetic appliances, equipment and services, such as home respiratory therapy, artificial limbs, orthopedic braces and therapeutic shoes, wheelchairs, powered mobility, crutches, canes, walkers, and other durable medical equipment and supplies.

VA will provide hearing aids and eyeglasses to Veterans who receive increased pension based on the need for regular aid and attendance or being permanently housebound; receive compensation for a service-connected disability; are former POWs or a Purple Heart award recipient.

Otherwise, hearing aids and eyeglasses are provided only in special circumstances, and not for normally occurring hearing or vision loss. For additional information, contact the Prosthetic Chief or Representative at the nearest VA health care facility or go to the web site: prosthetics.va.gov

Home Improvements and Structural Alterations

VA provides up to $4,100 lifetime benefit for service-connected veterans and up to $1,200 for non-service-connected veterans to make home improvements necessary for the continuation of treatment or for disability access to the home and essential lavatory and sanitary facilities.

Home Improvement and Structural Alterations grants provide for medically necessary improvements and/or structural changes to the Veteran's residence for the following purposes:

(1) Allowing entrance to, or exit from, the Veteran's residence.
(2) Use of essential lavatory and sanitary facilities.
(3) Allowing accessibility to kitchen or bathroom sinks or counters.
(4) Improving entrance paths or driveways in immediate area of the home to facilitate access to the home by the Veteran.

(5) Improving plumbing or electrical systems made necessary
due to installation of dialysis equipment in the home.

For application information, contact the prosthetic representative at
the nearest VA health care facility.

Special Eligibility Programs

Special Eligibility for Children with Spina Bifida: VA provides
needed health care benefits, including prosthetics, medical equipment, and supplies to certain children of Vietnam Veteran, i.e.,
children who are suffering from spina bifida or a disability associated
with such condition.

**Special Eligibility for Veterans Participating in Vocational Re-
habilitation:** Veterans participating in VA's vocational rehabilitation
program may receive VA health care benefits including prosthetics,
medical equipment, and supplies.

Limitations on Benefits Available to Veterans outside the U.S.:
Veterans outside the U.S. are eligible for prosthetics, medical equipment, and supplies only for a Service-connected disability.

Services for Blind and Visually Impaired Veterans

Blind veterans may be eligible for services at a VA medical center
or for admission to an inpatient or outpatient VA blind rehabilitation
program. In addition, blind veterans enrolled in the VA health care
system may receive:

1. A total health and benefits review as well as counseling on
   obtaining benefits that may be due to the veteran but have
   not been received.
2. Adjustment to blindness training and counseling.
3. Home improvements and structural alterations.
4. Specially adapted housing and adaptations.
5. Automobile grant.
6. Rehabilitation assessment and training to improve
   independence and quality of life.
7. Low-vision devices and training in their use.
8. Electronic and mechanical aids for the blind, including
   adaptive computers and computer-assisted devices such as
   reading machines and electronic travel aids.
9. Facilitation and recommendation for guide dogs and training

in the use of guide dogs.
10. Costs for veterinary care and equipment for guide dogs.
11. Talking books, tapes and Braille literature.
12. Family support.

Eligible visually impaired veterans (who are not blind) enrolled in the VA health care system may be eligible for services at a VA medical center or for admission to an outpatient VA blind rehabilitation program and may also receive:
1. A total health and benefits review.
2. Adjustment to vision loss counseling.
3. Rehabilitation assessment and training to improve independence and quality of life.
4. Low-vision devices and training in their use.
5. Electronic and mechanical aids for the visually impaired, including adaptive computers and computer-assisted devices, such as reading machines and electronic travel aids, and training in their use.
6. Family support.

Mental Health Care Treatment

Veterans eligible for VA medical care may apply for general mental health treatment including specialty services.Mental health services are available in specialty clinics, primary care clinics, nursing homes, and residential care facilities where veterans receive health care.

Specialized programs, such as mental health intensive case management, day centers, work programs and psychosocial rehabilitation are provided for those with serious mental health problems.

The list of services and programs that Mental Health supports include: inpatient care, residential care, outpatient mental health care, homeless programs, programs for incarcerated veterans, specialized PTSD services, military sexual trauma, psychosocial rehabilitation & recovery services, substance use disorders, suicide programs, geriatrics, violence prevention, evidence-based psychotherapy programs, mental health disaster response/post deployment activities

For more information on VA Mental Health services visit http://www.mentalhealth.va.gov/VAMentalHealthGroup.asp

Suicide Prevention Lifeline

Veterans experiencing an emotional distress/crisis or who need to talk to a trained mental health professional may call the National Suicide Prevention Lifeline toll-free lifeline number, 1-800-273-TALK (8255). The hotline is available 24 hours a day, seven days a week. Callers are immediately connected with a qualified and caring provider who can help.

On July 3, 2009, the VA launched a pilot on-line Chat Service, in partnership with Lifeline. The Veterans Chat Service is located at the VA National Suicide Prevention Hotline. Veterans Chat enables Veterans, their families and friends to go online where they can anonymously chat with a trained VA counselor. Veterans Chat can be accessed through the suicide prevention Web site www.suicidepreventionlifeline.org. by clicking on the Veterans Chat tab on the right side of the Web page.

Work Restoration Programs

VA provides vocational assistance and therapeutic work opportunities through several programs for veterans receiving VA health care. Each program offers treatment and rehabilitation services to help veterans live and work in their communities.

Participation in the following VA Work Restoration Programs cannot be used to deny or discontinue VA compensation or pension benefits. Payments received from Incentive Therapy and Compensated Work Therapy transitional work are not taxable.

Incentive Therapy (IT) provides a diversified work experience at VA medical centers for Veterans who exhibit severe mental illness and/ or physical impairments. IT services may consist of full or part time work with nominal remuneration limited to the maximum of one half of the Federal minimum wage.

CWT/ Sheltered Workshop (CWT) operates sheltered workshops at approximately 35 VA Medical Centers. CWT sheltered work shop is a pre-employment vocational activity that provides an opportunity for work hardening and assessment in a simulated work environment. Participating Veterans are paid on a piece rate basis.

CWT/Transitional Work (CWT/TW) is vocational assessment program that operates in VA medical centers and/or local community business and industry. CWT/TW participants are matched to real life work assignments for a time limited basis. Veterans are supervised by personnel of the sponsoring site, under the same job expectations experienced by non-CWT workers. CWT/TW participants are not considered employees and receive no traditional employee benefits.

Participants receive the greater of Federal or state minimum wage, or more depending on the type of work. Over forty percent of participants secure competitive employment at the time of discharge.

CWT/Supported Employment (CWT/SE) consists of full-time or part-time competitive employment with extensive clinical supports. The focus of CWT/SE is to assist Veterans with psychosis and other serious mental illness gain access to meaningful competitive employment. CWT/SE follow along support services are generally phased out after the Veteran is able to maintain employment independently.

Mental Health Residential Rehabilitation Treatment Program

Mental Health Residential Rehabilitation Treatment Programs (MH RRTP) (including Domiciliary RRTPs) provides residential rehabilitative and clinical care to Veterans who have a wide range of problems, illnesses, or rehabilitative care needs which can be medical, psychiatric, substance use, homelessness, vocational, educational, or social.

The MH RRTP provides a 24-hour therapeutic setting utilizing a milieu of peer and professional support. The programs provide a strong emphasis on psychosocial rehabilitation and recovery services that instill personal responsibility to achieve optimal levels of independence upon discharge to independent or supportive community living. MH RRTP also provides rehabilitative care for veterans who are homeless.

Eligibility: VA may provide domiciliary care to veterans whose annual gross household income does not exceed the maximum annual rate of VA pension or to veterans the Secretary of Veterans Affairs determines have no adequate means of support.

The copays for extended care services apply to domiciliary care.

Call your nearest benefits or health care facility to obtain the latest information.

Outpatient Dental Treatment

Veterans are eligible for outpatient dental treatment if they meet one of the following criteria:

If you:	You are eligible for:
Have a service-connected compensable dental disability or condition	Any needed dental care
Are a former prisoner of war	Any needed dental care
Have service-connected disabilities rated 100% disabling or are unemployable due to service-connected conditions	Any needed dental care
Are participating in a VA vocational rehabilitation program	Dental care needed to complete the program
Have a service connected and/or noncompensable dental condition or disability that existed at the time of discharge or release from a period of active duty of 90 days or more during the Persian Gulf War era	One-time dental care if you apply for dental care within 180 days of separation from active duty and your certificate of discharge does not indicate that all appropriate dental treatment had been rendered prior to discharge
Have a service-connected noncompensable dental condition or disability resulting from combat wounds or service trauma	You are eligible for needed care for the service-connected condition(s)
You have a dental condition clinically determined by VA to be currently aggravating a service-connected medical condition	You are eligible for dental care to resolve the problem
If you are receiving outpatient care or scheduled for inpatient care and require dental care for a condition complicating a medical condition currently under treatment	You are eligible for dental care to resolve the problem
Certain veterans enrolled in VA Homeless Program for 60 consecutive days or more	May receive basic outpatient dental services

For more information about eligibility for VA medical and dental benefits, contact the Health Benefits Service Center at 1-877-222-8387 or www.va.gov/healtheligibility/Library/pubs/Dental/Dental.pdf.

Nursing Home Care

VA provides nursing home services to veterans through three national programs: VA owned and operated Community Living Centers (CLC), state veterans' homes owned and operated by the states, and the contract community nursing home program. Each program has admission and eligibility criteria specific to the program.

VA Community Living Centers: Community Living Centers (CLC) provide a dynamic array of short stay (less than 90 days) and long stay (91 days or more) services. Short stay services include but are not limited to skilled nursing, respite care, rehabilitation, hospice, and maintenance care for veterans awaiting placement in the community. Short stay services are available for veterans who are enrolled in VA health care and require CLC services. Long stay services are available for enrolled veterans who need nursing home care for life or for an extended period of time for a service-connected disability, and those rated 60 percent service-connected and unemployable; or veterans or who have a 70 percent or greater service-connected disability. All others are based on available resources.

State Veterans' Home Program: State veterans homes are owned and operated by the states. The states petition VA for grant dollars for a portion of the construction costs followed by a request for recognition as a state home. Once recognized, VA pays a portion of the per diem if the state meets VA standards. States establish eligibility criteria and determine services offered for short and long-term care. Specialized services offered are dependent upon the capability of the home to render them.

Contract Community Nursing Home Program: VA health care facilities establish contracts with community nursing homes. The purpose of this program is to meet the nursing home needs of veterans who require long-term nursing home care in their own community, close to their families and meet the enrollment and eligibility requirements.

Admission Criteria: The general criteria for nursing home placement in each of the three programs requires that a resident must be medically stable, i.e. not acutely ill, have sufficient functional deficits to require inpatient nursing home care, and is assessed by an appropriate medical provider to be in need of institutional nursing home care. Furthermore, the veteran must meet the specific eligibility criteria for community living center care or the contract nursing home program and the eligibility criteria for the specific state veterans home.

Non-Institutional Long-term Care Services: In addition to nursing home care, VA offers a variety of other long-term care services either directly or by contract with community-based agencies. Such services include adult day health care, respite care, geriatric evaluation and management, hospice and palliative care, home based skilled nursing, and home based primary care. Veterans receiving these services may be subject to a copay .

Emergency Medical Care in U.S. Non-VA Facilities

In the case of medical emergencies, VA may reimburse or pay for emergency non-VA medical care not previously authorized that is provided to certain eligible Veterans when VA or other federal facilities are not feasibly available. This benefit may be dependent upon other conditions, such as notification to VA, the nature of treatment sought, the status of the Veteran, the presence of other health care insurance, and third party liability. Because there are different regulatory requirements that may affect VA payment and Veteran liability for the cost of care, it is very important that the nearest VA medical facility to where emergency services are furnished be notified as soon as possible after emergency treatment is sought. If emergency inpatient services are required, VA will assist in transferring the Veteran to a Department facility, if available. Claim timely filing limitations apply. For additional information, contact the nearest VA medical facility. Please note that reimbursement criteria for Veterans living or traveling outside the United States fall under VA's Foreign Medical Program (FMP), and differ from the criteria for payment of emergency treatment received in the United States. Please refer to the section below VA's Foreign Medical Program.

Foreign Medical Program

VA will pay for medical services for service-connected disabilities or any disability associated with and found to be aggravating a service-connected disability for those veterans living or traveling outside the United States. This program will also reimburse for the treatment of foreign medical services needed as part of an approved VA vocational rehabilitation program. Veterans living in the Philippines should register with the U.S. Veterans Affairs office in Pasay City, telephone 011-632-838-4566 or by email at manlopc.inqry@vba.va.gov. All other veterans living or planning to travel outside the U.S. should register with the Denver Foreign Medical Program office, P.O. Box 469061, Denver, CO 80246-9061, USA; telephone 303-331-7590. For information visit: www.va.gov/hac/forbeneficiaries/fmp/fmp.asp.

Some veterans traveling or living overseas can telephone the Foreign Medical Program toll free from these countries: Germany 0800-1800-011; Australia 1800-354-965; Italy 800-782-655; United Kingdom (England and Scotland) 0800-032-7425; Mexico 001-877-345-8179; Japan 00531-13-0871; Costa Rica 0800-013-0759; and Spain 900-981-776. (Note: Veterans in Mexico or Costa Rica must first dial the United States country code.)

Online Health Services

My HealtheVet (www.myhealth.va.gov) is VA's award-winning online Personal Health Record. Access is easy and convenient anywhere the Internet is available. My HealtheVet is for Veterans, active duty Service members, their dependents, and caregivers. With My HealtheVet users access trusted and secure VA health information to better manage their health care and facts about other VA benefits and services to which they may be entitled. My HealtheVet helps users to partner with their health care teams and provides them opportunities and tools to make informed decisions.

To register, simply go to www.myhealth.va.gov and follow the directions. Users can then record and track health information and history for their family and themselves; enter past and present military service events; keep activity and food journals; record, track, and graph vital signs; and, maintain other health measures.

Veterans enrolled at a VA health care facility can also access advanced features of My HealtheVet and can link their Personal Health Record with information from their VA electronic health record. To access the advanced features, Veterans must complete a one-time process called In-Person Authentication or "IPA." This includes making a visit to their VA facility to verify their identity in person. After completing the IPA, VA patients can use My HealtheVet to:
   • Refill their VA prescriptions by name, not just by the prescription number

- Record non-VA medications
- Receive VA Wellness Reminders
- Access new features as they become available

Expected in 2010, VA patients who complete the IPA also will see their VA appointments, VA lab test results, and VA list of allergies. They may also communicate with their health care teams through "Secure Messaging" as this feature becomes available at their local VA facility.

Register for My HealtheVet today at www.myhealth.va.gov. If you are a VA patient and want to access advanced features, don't forget to complete the one-time IPA process which takes only a few minutes. Start now and benefit from using My HealtheVet. It's quick, easy and it's for you. My HealtheVet: 24/7 Access to VA Health Care Services and Information.

Chapter 2
Service-Connected Disabilities

Disability Compensation
Disability compensation is a monetary benefit paid to veterans who are disabled by an injury or illness that was incurred or aggravated during active military service. These disabilities are considered to be service-connected.

Disability compensation varies with the degree of disability and the number of a veteran's dependents, and is paid monthly. Veterans with certain severe disabilities may be eligible for additional special monthly compensation. The benefits are not subject to federal or state income tax.

The payment of military retirement pay, disability severance pay and separation incentive payments, known as SSB (Special Separation Benefits) and VSI (Voluntary Separation Incentives) affects the amount of VA compensation paid to disabled veterans.

To be eligible, the service of the veteran must have been terminated through separation or discharge under conditions other than dishonorable. For additional details, visit the Web site at www.vba.va.gov/bln/21/.

Receiving Disability Benefit Payments
VA offers three disability benefit payment options. Most veterans receive their payments by direct deposit to a bank, savings and loan or credit union account.

In some areas, veterans who do not have a bank account can open a federally insured Electronic Transfer Account, which costs about $3 a month, provides a monthly statement, and allows for cash withdrawals.

Other veterans may choose to receive benefits by check. To choose or change a payment method, call toll-free 1-877-838-2778, Monday through Friday, 7:30 a.m. - 4:50 p.m., CST.

2010 VA Disability Compensation Rates for Veterans

Veteran's Disability Rating	Monthly Rate Paid to Veterans
10 percent	$123
20 percent	$243
30 percent*	$376
40 percent*	$541
50 percent*	$770
60 percent*	$974
70 percent*	$1,228
80 percent*	$1,427
90 percent*	$1,604
100 percent*	$2,673

*Veterans with disability ratings of at least 30 percent are eligible for additional allowances for dependents, including spouses, minor children, children between the ages of 18 and 23 who are attending school, children who are permanently incapable of self-support because of a disability arising before age 18, and dependent parents. The additional amount depends on the disability rating and the number of dependents.

Presumptive Conditions for Disability Compensation
All veterans who develop Amyotrophic Lateral Sclerosis (ALS), also known as Lou Gehrig's Disease, at any time after separation from service may be eligible for compensation for that disability.

Certain veterans are eligible for disability compensation based on the presumption that their disability is service-connected

Prisoners of War: For former POWs who were imprisoned for any length of time, the following disabilities are presumed to be service-connected if they are rated at least 10 percent disabling anytime after military service: psychosis, any of the anxiety states, dysthymic disorder, organic residuals of frostbite, post-traumatic osteoarthritis, heart disease or hypertensive vascular disease and their complications, stroke, residuals of stroke and effective October 10, 2008, osteoporosis if the veteran has post-traumatic stress disorder (PTSD).

For former POWs who were imprisoned for at least 30 days, the following conditions are also presumed to be service-connected: avitaminosis, beriberi, chronic dysentery, helminthiasis, malnutrition (including optic atrophy), pellagra and/or other nutritional deficiencies, irritable bowel syndrome, peptic ulcer disease, peripheral neuropathy, cirrhosis of the liver and effective September 28, 2009, osteoporosis.

Veterans Exposed to Agent Orange and Other Herbicides: A veteran who served in the Republic of Vietnam between Jan. 9, 1962, and May 7, 1975, is presumed to have been exposed to Agent Orange and other herbicides used in support of military operations.

Twelve illnesses are presumed by VA to be service-connected for such veterans: chloracne or other acneform disease similar to chloracne, porphyria cutanea tarda, soft-tissue sarcoma (other than osteosarcoma, chondrosarcoma, Kaposi's sarcoma or mesothelioma), Hodgkin's disease, multiple myeloma, respiratory cancers (lung, bronchus, larynx, trachea), non-Hodgkin's lymphoma, prostate cancer, acute and subacute peripheral neuropathy, diabetes mellitus (Type 2), chronic lymphocytic leukemia and AL amyloidosis..

Veterans Exposed to Radiation: For veterans who participated in "radiation risk activities" as defined in VA regulations while on active duty, active duty for training, or inactive duty training, the following conditions are presumed to be service-connected: all forms of leukemia (except for chronic lymphocytic leukemia); cancer of the thyroid, breast, pharynx, esophagus, stomach, small intestine, pancreas, bile ducts, gall bladder, salivary gland, urinary tract (renal pelvis, ureter, urinary bladder and urethra), brain, bone, lung, colon, and ovary, bronchiolo-alveolar carcinoma, multiple myeloma, lymphomas (other than Hodgkin's disease), and primary liver cancer (except if cirrhosis or hepatitis B is indicated).

To determine service connection for other conditions or exposures not eligible for presumptive service connection, VA considers factors such as the amount of radiation exposure, duration of exposure, elapsed time between exposure and onset of the disease, gender and family history, age at time of exposure, the extent to which a non service-related exposure could contribute to disease, and the relative sensitivity of exposed tissue.

Gulf War Veterans with Chronic Disabilities may receive disability compensation for chronic disabilities resulting from undiagnosed illnesses and/or medically unexplained chronic multi-symptom illnesses defined by a cluster of signs or symptoms. A disability is considered chronic if it has existed for at least six months.

The undiagnosed illnesses must have appeared either during active service in the Southwest Asia Theater of Operations during the Gulf War period of Aug. 2, 1990, to July 31, 1991, or to a degree of at least 10 percent at any time since then through Dec. 31, 2011. This theater of operations includes Iraq, Kuwait, Saudi Arabia, the neutral zone between Iraq and Saudi Arabia, Bahrain, Qatar, the United Arab Emirates, Oman, the Gulf of Aden, the Gulf of Oman, the Persian Gulf, the Arabian Sea, the Red Sea, and the airspace above these locations.

The following are examples of symptoms of an undiagnosed illness: chronic fatigue syndrome, fibromyalgia, skin disorders, headache, muscle pain, joint pain, neurological symptoms, neuropsychological symptoms, symptoms involving the respiratory system, sleep disturbances, gastrointestinal symptoms, cardiovascular symptoms, abnormal weight loss, and menstrual disorders.

Concurrent Retirement and Disability Payments (CRDP) restores retired pay on a graduated 10-year schedule for retirees with a 50 to 90 percent VA-rated disability. Concurrent retirement payments increase 10 percent per year through 2013. Veterans rated 100 percent disabled by VA are entitled to full CRDP without being phased in. Veterans receiving benefits at the 100 percent rate due to individual unemployability are entitled to full CRDP effective Jan. 1, 2005..

Eligibility: To qualify, veterans must also meet all three of the following criteria:
1. Have 20 or more years of active duty, or full-time National Guard duty, or satisfactory service as a reservist, or
2. Be in a retired status.
3. Be receiving retired pay (must be offset by VA payments).
Retirees do not need to apply for this benefit. Payment is coordinated between VA and the Department of Defense (DoD).

Combat-Related Special Compensation (CRSC) provides tax-free monthly payments to eligible retired veterans with combat-related injuries. With CRSC, veterans can receive both their full military retirement pay and their VA disability compensation if the injury is combat-related.

Eligibility: Retired veterans with combat-related injuries must meet all of the following criteria to apply for CRSC:
1. Active or Reserve component with 20 years of creditable service or medically retired.
2. Receiving military retired pay.
3. Have a 10 percent or greater VA-rated injury.
4. Military retired pay is reduced by VA disability payments (VA Waiver).

In addition, veterans must be able to provide documentary evidence that their injuries were a result of one of the following:
- Training that simulates war (e.g., exercises, field training)
- Hazardous duty (e.g., flight, diving, parachute duty)
- An instrumentality of war (e.g. combat vehicles, weapons, Agent Orange)
- Armed conflict (e.g. gunshot wounds, Purple Heart)

For information, visit www.defenselink.mil, or call the toll free phone number for the veteran's branch of service: (Army) 1-866-281-3254; (Air Force) 1-800-616-3775; (Navy) 1-877-366-2772. The Army has its own Web site at https://www.hrc.army.mil/site/crsc/index.html and e-mail at crsc.info@us.army.mil.

Programs for Service-Connected Disabilities

Vocational Rehabilitation and Employment (VR&E) Program assists veterans who have service-connected disabilities obtain and maintain suitable employment. Independent living services are also available for severely disabled veterans who are not currently ready to seek employment. Additional information is available on VA's Web site at www.vetsuccess.gov.

Eligibility: A veteran must have a VA service-connected disability rated at least 20 percent with an employment handicap, or rated 10 percent with a serious employment handicap, and be discharged or released from military service under other than dishonorable conditions. Servicemembers pending medical separation from active duty may also apply if their disabilities are reasonably expected to be rated at least 20 percent following their discharge.

Entitlement: A VA counselor must decide if the individual has an employment handicap based upon the results of a comprehensive evaluation. After an entitlement decision is made, the individual and counselor will work together to develop a rehabilitation plan. The rehabilitation plan will specify the rehabilitation services to be provided.

Services: Rehabilitation services provided to participants in the VR&E program are under one of five tracks. VA pays the cost of approved training that is included in an individual's rehabilitation plan. Subsistence allowance may also be provided. The tracks are:

Reemployment with Previous Employer: For individuals who are separating from active duty or in the National Guard or Reserves and are returning to work for their previous employer.

Rapid Access to Employment: For individuals who either wish to obtain employment soon after separation or who already have the necessary skills to be competitive in the job market in an appropriate occupation.

Self-Employment: For individuals who have limited access to traditional employment, need flexible work schedules, or who require more accommodation in the work environment due to their disabling conditions or other life circumstances.

Employment Through Long-Term Services: For individuals who need specialized training and/or education to obtain and maintain suitable employment.

Independent Living Services: For veterans who are not currently able to work and need rehabilitation services to live more independently.

Period of a Rehabilitation Program: Generally, veterans must complete a program within 12 years from their separation from military service or within 12 years from the date VA notifies them that they have a compensable service-connected disability. Depending

on the length of program needed, veterans may be provided up to
48 months of full-time services or their part-time equivalent. These
limitations may be extended in certain circumstances.

Work-Study: Veterans training at the three-quarter or full-time rate
may participate in VA's work-study program and provide VA outreach services, prepare/process VA paperwork, work at a VA medical facility, or perform other VA-approved activities. A portion of the
work-study allowance equal to 40 percent of the total may be paid in
advance.

Specially Adapted Housing Grants

Certain veterans and servicemembers with service-connected disabilities may be entitled to a Specially Adapted Housing (SAH) grant
from VA to help build a new specially adapted house, to adapt a
home they already own, or buy a house and modify it to meet their
disability-related requirements. Eligible veterans or servicemembers
may now receive up to three grants, with the total dollar amount of
the grants not to exceed the maximum allowable. Previous grant
recipients who had received assistance of less than the current maximum allowable may be eligible for an additional SAH grant.

Eligibility for up to $63,780: VA may approve a grant of not more
than 50 percent of the cost of building, buying, or adapting existing homes or paying to reduce indebtedness on a currently owned
home that is being adapted, up to a maximum of $63,780. In certain
instances, the full grant amount may be applied toward remodeling
costs. Veterans and servicemembers must be determined eligible
to receive compensation for permanent and total service-connected
disability due to one of the following:

1. Loss or loss of use of both lower extremities, such as to
   preclude locomotion without the aid of braces, crutches,
   canes or a wheelchair.
2. Loss or loss of use of both upper extremities at or above the
   elbow.
3. Blindness in both eyes, having only light perception, plus loss
   or loss of use of one lower extremity
4. Loss or loss of use of one lower extremity together with (a)
   residuals of organic disease or injury, or (b) the loss or loss of
   use of one upper extremity which so affects the functions of
   balance or propulsion as to preclude locomotion without the
   use of braces, canes, crutches or a wheelchair.
5. Severe burn injuries

Eligibility for up to $12,756: VA may approve a grant for the cost, up to a maximum of $12,756, for necessary adaptations to a veteran's or servicemember's residence or to help them acquire a residence already adapted with special features for their disability, to purchase and adapt a home, or for adaptations to a family member's home in which they will reside.

To be eligible for this grant, veterans and servicemembers must be entitled to compensation for permanent and total service-connected disability due to one of the following:
1. Blindness in both eyes with 5/200 visual acuity or less.
2. Anatomical loss or loss of use of both hands.
3. Severe burn injuries.

Eligible veterans and servicemembers who are temporarily residing in a home owned by a family member may also receive a Temporary Residence Adaptation (TRA) grant to help the veteran or servicemember adapt the family member's home to meet his or her special needs. Those eligible for a $63,780 grant would be permitted to use up to $14,000 and those eligible for a $12,756 grant would be permitted to use up to $2,000. Grant amounts will also be adjusted annually based on a cost-of-construction index.

The first adjustment occurred on Oct. 1, 2009, with future adjustments each Oct. 1 thereafter. These adjustments will increase the grant amounts or leave them unchanged; they will not decrease the grant amounts. The maximum amount for a TRA grant is not indexed and remains unchanged.

The property may be located outside the United States, in a country or political subdivision which allows individuals to have or acquire a beneficial property interest, and in which the Secretary of Veterans Affairs, in his or her discretion, has determined that it is reasonably practicable for the Secretary to provide assistance in acquiring specially adapted housing. For more information on the use of such grants, contact Brian Bixler, Specially Adapted Housing, at 202-461-9546 or via e-mail at brian.bixler@va.gov.

Supplemental Financing: Veterans and servicemembers with available loan guaranty entitlement may also obtain a guaranteed loan or a direct loan from VA to supplement the grant to acquire a specially adapted home. Amounts with a guaranteed loan from a private lender will vary, but the maximum direct loan from VA is $33,000. Additional information about the Specially Adapted Housing Program is available on VA's Web site at www.homeloans.va.gov/sah.htm.

Automobile Allowance

Veterans and servicemembers may be eligible for a one-time payment of not more than $11,000 toward the purchase of an automobile or other conveyance if they have service-connected loss or permanent loss of use of one or both hands or feet, permanent impairment of vision of both eyes to a certain degree, or ankylosis (immobility) of one or both knees or one or both hips.

They may also be eligible for adaptive equipment, and for repair, replacement, or reinstallation required because of disability or for the safe operation of a vehicle purchased with VA assistance. To apply, contact a VA regional office at 1-800-827-1000 or the nearest VA health care facility.

Clothing Allowance

Any veteran who is service-connected for a disability for which he or she uses prosthetic or orthopedic appliances may receive an annual clothing allowance. This allowance also is available to any veteran whose service-connected skin condition requires prescribed medication that irreparably damages outer garments. To apply, contact the prosthetic representative at the nearest VA medical center.

Aid and Attendance for Housebound Veterans

A veteran who is determined by VA to be in need of the regular aid and attendance of another person, or a veteran who is permanently housebound, may be entitled to additional disability compensation or pension payments. A veteran evaluated at 30 percent or more disabled is entitled to receive an additional payment for a spouse who is in need of the aid and attendance of another person.

Vocational Rehabilitation & Employment Rates

In some cases, a veteran requires additional education or training to become employable. A subsistence allowance is paid each month during training and is based on the rate of attendance (full-time or part-time), the number of dependents, and the type of training. The charts below show the rates as of Oct. 1, 2009.

Subsistence allowance is paid at the following monthly rates for training in an institution of higher learning.

Training Time	Veterans With No Dependents	Veterans With One Dependent	Veterans With Two Dependents	Additional Dependent
Full-time	$547.54	$679.18	$800.36	$58.34
3/4-time	$411.41	$510.12	$598.38	$44.86
1/2-time	$275.28	$341.07	$400.92	$29.93

Subsistence allowance is paid at the following monthly rates for full-time training only in non-pay or nominal pay on-the-job training in a federal, state, local or federally recognized Indian tribe agency; training in the home; and vocational training in a rehabilitation facility or sheltered workshop.

Training Time	Veterans With No Dependents	Veterans With One Dependent	Veterans With Two Dependents	Additional Dependent
Full-time	$547.54	$679.18	$800.36	$58.34

Subsistence allowance is paid at the following monthly rates for full-time training only in farm cooperative, apprenticeship, and other on-job training. Payments are variable, based on the wages received. The maximum rates are:

Training Time	Veterans With No Dependents	Veterans With One Dependent	Veterans With Two Dependents	Additional Dependent
Full-time	$478.73	$578.92	$667.21	$43.40

Subsistence allowance is paid at the following monthly rates for non-pay or nominal pay work experience in a federal, state, local or federally recognized Indian tribe agency.

Training Time	Veterans With No Dependents	Veterans With One Dependent	Veterans With Two Dependents	Additional Dependent
Full-time	$547.54	$679.18	$800.36	$58.34
3/4-time	$411.41	$510.41	$598.38	$44.86
1/2-time	$275.28	$341.07	$400.92	$29.93

Subsistence allowance is paid at the following monthly rates for training programs that include a combination of institutional and on-job training.

Greater Than Half-Time	Veterans With No Dependents	Veterans With One Dependent	Veterans With Two Dependents	Additional Dependent
Institutional	$547.54	$679.18	$800.36	$58.34
On-job	$478.73	$578.92	$667.21	$43.40

Subsistence allowance is paid at the following monthly rates for full-time training only for non-farm cooperative institutional training and non-farm cooperative on-job training.

Training Time	Veterans With No Dependents	Veterans With One Dependent	Veterans With Two Dependents	Additional Dependent
Institutiontional	$547.54	$679.18	$800.36	$58.34
On-job	$478.73	$578.92	$667.21	$43.40

Subsistence allowance is paid at the following monthly rates during the period of enrollment in a rehabilitation facility when a veteran is pursuing an approved independent living program plan.

Training Time	Veterans With No Dependents	Veterans With One Dependent	Veterans With Two Dependents	Additional Dependent
Full-time	$547.54	$679.18	$800.36	$58.34
3/4-time	$411.41	$510.12	$598.38	$44.86
1/2–time	$275.28	$341.07	$400.92	$29.93

Subsistence allowance is paid at the following monthly rates during the period of enrollment in a rehabilitation facility when a veteran requires this service for the purpose of extended evaluation.

Training Time	Veterans With No Dependents	Veterans With One Dependent	Veterans With Two Dependents	Additional Dependent
Full-time	$547.54	$679.18	$800.36	$58.34
3/4-time	$411.41	$510.12	$598.38	$44.86
1/2-time	$275.28	$341.07	$400.92	$29.93
1/4–time	$137.62	$170.55	$200.45	$14.93

Chapter 3
VA Pensions

Eligibility for Disability Pension

Veterans with low incomes who are either permanently and totally disabled, or age 65 and older, may be eligible for monetary support if they have 90 days or more of active military service, at least one day of which was during a period of war. (Veterans who entered active duty on or after Sept. 8, 1980, or officers who entered active duty on or after Oct. 16, 1981, may have to meet a longer minimum period of active duty). The veteran's discharge must have been under conditions other than dishonorable and the disability must be for reasons other than the veteran's own willful misconduct.

Payments are made to bring the veteran's total income, including other retirement or Social Security income, to a level set by Congress. Un-reimbursed medical expenses may reduce countable income for VA purposes.

Protected Pension

Pension beneficiaries, who were receiving a VA pension on Dec. 31, 1978, and do not wish to elect the Improved Pension, will continue to receive the pension rate received on that date. This rate generally continues as long as the beneficiary's income remains within established limits, or net worth does not bar payment, and the beneficiary does not lose any dependents.

Beneficiaries must continue to meet basic eligibility factors, such as permanent and total disability for veterans. VA must adjust rates for other reasons, such as a veteran's hospitalization in a VA facility.

Medal of Honor Pension

VA administers pensions to recipients of the Medal of Honor. Congress set the monthly pension at $1,194.

Improved Disability Pension

Congress establishes the maximum annual improved disability pension rates. Payments are reduced by the amount of countable income of the veteran, spouse and dependent children. When a veteran without a spouse or a child is furnished nursing home or domiciliary care by VA, the pension is reduced to an amount not to exceed $90 per month after three calendar months of care. The reduction may be delayed if nursing-home care is being continued to provide the veteran with rehabilitation services.

2010 VA Improved Disability Pension Rates

Status of Veteran's Family Situation and Caretaking Needs	Maximum Annual Rate
Veteran without dependents	$11,830
Veteran with one dependent	$15,493
Veteran permanently housebound, no dependents	$14,457
Veteran permanently housebound, one dependent	$18,120
Veteran needing regular aid and attendance, no dependents	$19,736
Veteran needing regular aid and attendance, one dependent	$23,396
Two veterans married to one another	$15,493
Increase for each additional dependent child	$2,020

* Additional information can be found in the Compensation and Pension Benefits section of VA's Internet pages at www.vba.va.gov/bln/21/index.htm.

Chapter 4

Education and Training

This chapter provides a summary of VA educational and training benefits. Additional information can be found at www.gibill.va.gov/ or by calling 1-888-GI-BILL-1 (1-888-442-4551).

Post – 9/11 GI Bill

Eligibility: The Post- 9/11 GI Bill is a new education benefit program for servicemembers and veterans who served on active duty on or after Sept.11, 2001. Benefits are payable for training pursued on or after Aug. 1, 2009. No payments can be made under this program for training pursued before that date.

To be eligible, the servicemember or veteran must serve at least 90 aggregate days on active duty after Sept. 10, 2001, and remain on active duty or be honorably:

1. Discharged from active duty status;
2. Released from active duty and placed on the retired list or temporary disability retired list;
3. Released from active duty and transferred to the Fleet Reserve or Fleet Marine Corps Reserve;
4. Released from active duty for further service in a reserve component of the Armed Forces.

Veterans may also be eligible if they were honorably discharged from active duty for a service-connected disability after serving 30 continuous days after Sept. 10, 2001.Generally, servicemembers or veterans may receive up to 36 months of entitlement under the Post-9/11 GI Bill.

Eligibility for benefits expires 15 years from the last period of active duty of at least 90 consecutive days. If released for a service-connected disability after at least 30 days of continuous service, eligibility ends 15 years from when the member is released for the service-connected disability.

If, on Aug.1, 2009, the servicemember or veteran is eligible for the Montgomery GI Bill; the Montgomery GI Bill – Selected Reserve; or the Reserve Educational Assistance Program, and qualifies for the Post-9/11 GI Bill, an irrevocable election must be made to receive benefits under the Post-9/11 GI Bill.

In most instances, once the election to receive benefits under the Post-9/11 GI Bill is made, the individual will no longer be eligible to receive benefits under the relinquished program.

Based on the length of active duty service, eligible participants are entitled to receive a percentage of the following:

1. Cost of tuition and fees, not to exceed the most expensive in-state undergraduate tuition at a public institution of higher education (paid directly to the school);
2. Monthly housing allowance equal to the basic allowance for housing payable to a military E-5 with dependents, in the same zip code as the primary school (paid directly to the servicemember or veteran);
3. Yearly books and supplies stipend of up to $1000 per year (paid directly to the servicemember or veteran); and
4. A one-time payment of $500 paid to certain individuals relocating from highly rural areas.

   * The housing allowance and books and supplies stipend are not payable to individuals on active duty. The housing allowance is not payable to those pursuing training at half time or less or to individuals enrolled solely in distance learning programs.

Benefits may be used for any approved program offered by a school in the United States that is authorized to grant an associate (or higher) degree. Call 1-888-442-4551 or visit www.gibill.va.gov for information about attending school in a foreign country.

If entitlement to the Post-9/11 GI Bill was the result of transferring from the Montgomery GI Bill; the Montgomery GI Bill – Selected Reserve; or the Reserve Education Assistance Program, recipients may also receive Post-9/11 GI Bill benefits for flight training, apprenticeship or on-the-job training programs, and correspondence courses. Individuals serving an aggregate period of active duty after Sept. 10, 2001 can receive the following percentages based on length of service:

Active duty service	Maximum Benefit
At least 36 months	100%
At least 30 continuous days and discharged due to service-connected disability	100%
At least 30 months < 36 months	90%
At least 24 months < 30 months	80%
At least 18 months < 24 months	70%
At least 12 months < 18 months	60%
At least 6 months < 12 months	50%
At least 90 days < 6 months	40%

Transfer of Entitlement (TOE): DOD may offer members of the Armed Forces on or after Aug.1, 2009, the opportunity to transfer benefits to a spouse or dependent children. DOD and the military services must approve all requests for this benefit. Members of the Armed Forces approved for the TOE may only transfer any unused portion of their Post-9/11 GI Bill benefits while a member of the Armed Forces, subject to their period of eligibility.

The Yellow Ribbon G.I. Education Enhancement Program was enacted to potentially assist eligible individuals with payment of their tuition and fees in instances where costs exceed the most expensive in-state undergraduate tuition at a public institution of higher educa-tion. To be eligible, the student must be: a veteran receiving benefits at the 100% benefit rate payable, a transfer-of-entitlement-eligible dependent child, or a transfer-of-entitlement eligible spouse of a veteran. The school of attendance must have accepted VA's invita-tion to participate in the program, state how much student tuition will be waived (up to 50%) and how many participants will be accepted into the program during the current academic year. VA will match the school's percentage (up to 50%) to reduce or eliminate out-of-pocket costs for eligible participants.

Work-Study Program: Veterans and eligible transfer-of-entitlement recipients who train at the three-quarter rate of pursuit or higher may be eligible for a work-study program in which they work for VA and receive hourly wages. Students under the work-study program

must be supervised by a VA employee and all duties performed must relate to VA. The types of work allowed include:
1. VA paperwork processing at schools or other training facilities.
2. Assistance with patient care at VA hospitals or domiciliary care facilities.
3. Work at national or state veterans' cemeteries.
4. Various jobs within any VA regional office.
5. Other VA-approved activities.

Marine Gunnery Sergeant John David Fry Scholarship: This scholarship entitles children of those who die in the line of duty on or since September 11, 2001, to use Post-9/11 GI Bill benefits.

Eligible children:
• are entitled to 36 months of benefits at the 100% level
• have 15 years to use the benefit beginning on their 18th birthday
• may use the benefit until their 33rd birthday
• are not eligible for the Yellow Ribbon Program

Educational and Vocational Counseling Services: Refer to Chapter 10, "Transition Assistance", for detailed information on available services.

Montgomery GI Bill

Eligibility: VA educational benefits may be used while the servicemember is on active duty or after the servicemember's separation from active duty with a fully honorable military discharge. Discharges "under honorable conditions" and "general" discharges do not establish eligibility.

Eligibility generally expires 10 years after the servicemember's discharge. However, there are exceptions for disability, re-entering active duty, and upgraded discharges.

All participants must have a high school diploma, equivalency certificate, or have completed 12 hours toward a college degree before applying for benefits.

Previously, servicemembers had to meet the high school requirement before they completed their initial active duty obligation. Those who did not may now meet the requirement and reapply for benefits. If eligible, they must use their benefits either within 10 years from the date of last discharge from active duty or by Nov. 2, 2010, whichever is later.

Additionally, every veteran must establish eligibility under one of four categories.

Category 1: Service after June 30, 1985
For veterans who entered active duty for the first time after June 30, 1985, did not decline MGIB in writing, and had their military pay reduced by $100 a month for 12 months. Servicemembers can apply after completing two continuous years of service. Veterans must have completed three continuous years of active duty, or two continuous years of active duty if they first signed up for less than three years or have an obligation to serve four years in the Selected Reserve (the 2x4 program) and enter the Selected Reserve within one year of discharge.

Servicemembers or veterans who received a commission as a result of graduation from a service academy or completion of an ROTC scholarship are not eligible under Category 1 unless they received their commission:
    1. After becoming eligible for MGIB benefits (including completing the minimum service requirements for the initial period of active duty); or
    2. After Sept.30, 1996, and received less than $3,400 during any one year under ROTC scholarship.

Servicemembers or veterans who declined MGIB because they received repayment from the military for education loans are also ineligible under Category 1. If they did not decline MGIB and received loan repayments, the months served to repay the loans will be deducted from their entitlement.

Early Separation from Military Service: Servicemembers who did not complete the required period of military service may be eligible under

Category 1: If discharged for one of the following:
    1. Convenience of the government—with 30 continuous months of service for an obligation of three or more years, or 20

continuous months of service for an obligation of less than
three years
2. Service-connected disability
3. Hardship
4. A medical condition diagnosed prior to joining the military.
5. A condition that interfered with performance of duty and did
   not result from misconduct
6. A reduction in force (in most cases).
7. Sole Survivorship (if discharged after 9/11/01)

Category 2: Vietnam Era GI Bill Conversion
For veterans who had remaining entitlement under the Vietnam Era
GI Bill on Dec. 31, 1989, and served on active duty for any number
of days during the period Oct. 19, 1984, to June 30, 1985, for at least
three continuous years beginning on July 1, 1985; or at least two
continuous years of active duty beginning on July 1, 1985, followed
by four years in the Selected Reserve beginning within one year of
release from active duty.

Veterans not on active duty on Oct. 19, 1984, may be eligible under Category 2 if they served three continuous years on active duty
beginning on or after July 1, 1985, or two continuous years of active
duty at any time followed by four continuous years in the Selected
Reserve beginning within one year of release from active duty.

Veterans are barred from eligibility under Category 2 if they received
a commission after Dec. 31, 1976, as a result of graduation from a
service academy or completion of an ROTC scholarship.

However, such a commission is not a disqualifier if they received the
commission after becoming eligible for MGIB benefits, or received
the commission after Sept.30, 1996, and received less than $3,400
during any one year under ROTC scholarship.

Category 3: Involuntary Separation/Special Separation
For veterans who meet one of the following requirements:
   1. Elected MGIB before being involuntarily separated; or
   2. Owere voluntarily separated under the Voluntary Separation
      Incentive or the Special Separation Benefit program, elected
      MGIB benefits before being separated, and had military pay
      reduced by $1,200 before discharge.

Category 4: Veterans Educational Assistance Program
For veterans who participated in the Veterans Educational Assistance Program (VEAP) and:
    1. Served on active duty on Oct. 9, 1996.
    2. Participated in VEAP and contributed money to an account.
    3. Elected MGIB by Oct. 9, 1997, and paid $1,200.

Veterans who participated in VEAP on or before Oct. 9, 1996, may also be eligible even if they did not deposit money in a VEAP account if they served on active duty from Oct. 9, 1996, through April 1, 2000, elected MGIB by Oct. 31, 2001, and contributed $2,700 to MGIB.

Certain National Guard service members may also qualify under Category 4 if they:
    1. Served for the first time on full-time active duty in the National Guard between June 30, 1985, and Nov. 29, 1989, and had no previous active duty service.
    2. Elected MGIB during the nine-month window ending on July 9, 1997; and
    3. Paid $1,200.

Payments: Effective Oct. 1, 2009, the rate for full-time training in college, technical or vocational school is $1,368 a month for those who served three years or more or two years plus four years in the Selected Reserve. For those who served less than three years, the monthly rate is $1,111.

Benefits are reduced for part-time training. Payments for other types of training follow different rules. VA will pay an additional amount, called a "kicker" or "college fund," if directed by DOD. Visit www.gibill.va.gov for more information.

The maximum number of months veterans can receive payments is 36 months at the full-time rate or the part-time equivalent.

The following groups qualify for the maximum: veterans who served the required length of active duty, veterans with an obligation of three years or more who were separated early for the convenience of the government and served 30 continuous months, and veterans with an obligation of less than three years who were separated early for the convenience of the government and served 20 continuous months.

Types of Training Available:
1. Courses at colleges and universities leading to associate, bachelor or graduate degrees, including accredited independent study offered through distance education.
2. Courses leading to a certificate or diploma from business, technical or vocational schools.
3. Apprenticeship or on-the-job training for those not on active duty, including self-employment training begun on or after June 16, 2004, for ownership or operation of a franchise
4. Correspondence courses, under certain conditions.
5. Flight training, if the veteran holds a private pilot's license upon beginning the training and meets the medical requirements.
6. State-approved teacher certification programs.
7. Preparatory courses necessary for admission to a college or graduate school.
8. License and certification tests approved for veterans.
9. Entrepreneurship training courses to create or expand small businesses.
10. Tuition assistance using MGIB as "Top-Up" (active duty service members).

Accelerated payments for certain high-cost programs are authorized.

Work-Study Program: Veterans who train at the three-quarter or full-time rate may be eligible for a work-study program in which they work for VA and receive hourly wages.

Students under the work-study program must be supervised by a VA employee and all duties performed must relate to VA. The types of work allowed include:
1. VA paperwork processing at schools or other training facilities.
2. Assistance with patient care at VA hospitals or domiciliary care facilities.
3. Work at national or state veterans' cemeteries.
4. Various jobs within any VA regional office.
5. Other VA-approved activities.

Educational and Vocational Counseling Services: Refer to Chapter 10, "Transition Assistance", for detailed information on available services.

Veterans' Educational Assistance Program

Eligibility: Active duty personnel could participate in the Veterans' Educational Assistance Program (VEAP) if they entered active duty for the first time after Dec. 31, 1976, and before July 1, 1985, and made a contribution prior to April 1, 1987.

The maximum contribution is $2,700. Active duty participants may make a lump-sum contribution to their VEAP account. For more information, visit the Web site at www.gibill.va.gov.

Servicemembers who participated in VEAP are eligible to receive benefits while on active duty if:
1. At least 3 months of contributions are available, except for high school or elementary, in which only one month is needed.
2. And they enlisted for the first time after Sept. 7, 1980, and completed 24 months of their first period of active duty.

Servicemembers must receive a discharge under conditions other than dishonorable for the qualifying period of service. Servicemembers who enlisted for the first time after Sept.7, 1980, or entered active duty as an officer or enlistee after Oct. 16, 1981, must have completed 24 continuous months of active duty, unless they meet a qualifying exception.

Eligibility generally expires 10 years from release from active duty, but can be extended under special circumstances.

Payments: DOD will match contributions at the rate of $2 for every $1 put into the fund and may make additional contributions, or "kickers," as necessary. For training in college, vocational or technical schools, the payment amount depends on the type and hours of training pursued. The maximum amount is $300 a month for full-time training.

Training, Work-Study, Counseling: VEAP participants may receive the same training, work-study benefits and counseling as provided under the MGIB.

Chapter 5

Home Loan Guaranty

VA home loan guaranties are issued to help eligible servicemembers, veterans, reservists and unmarried surviving spouses obtain homes, condominiums, residential cooperative housing units, and manufactured homes, and to refinance loans. For additional information or to obtain VA loan guaranty forms, visit www.homeloans.va.gov/.

Loan Uses: A VA guaranty helps protect lenders from loss if the borrower fails to repay the loan. It can be used to obtain a loan to:
1. Buy or build a home.
2. Buy a residential condominium unit.
3. Buy a residential cooperative housing unit.
4. Repair, alter, or improve a residence owned by the veteran and occupied as a home.
5. Refinance an existing home loan.
6. Buy a manufactured home and/or lot.
7. Install a solar heating or cooling system or other energy-efficient improvements.

Eligibility: In addition to the periods of eligibility and conditions of service requirements, applicants must have a good credit rating, sufficient income, a valid Certificate of Eligibility (COE), and agree to live in the property in order to be approved by a lender for a VA home loan.

To obtain a COE, complete VA Form 26-1880 -- "Request for a Certificate of Eligibility" -- and mail to: VA Eligibility Center, P.O. Box 20729, Winston-Salem, NC 27120.

It is also possible to obtain a COE from your lender. Most lenders have access to VA's "WebLGY" system. This Internet-based application can establish eligibility and issue an online COE in seconds. Not all cases can be processed online – only those for which VA has sufficient data in its records. However, veterans are encouraged to ask their lenders about this method of obtaining a COE before sending an application to the Eligibility Center. For more information, visit www.homeloans.va.gov/eligibility.htm.

Periods of Eligibility: World War II: (1) active duty service after Sept.15, 1940, and prior to July 26, 1947; (2) discharge under other than dishonorable conditions; and (3) at least 90 days total service unless discharged early for a service-connected disability.

Post-World War II period: (1) active duty service after July 25, 1947, and prior to June 27, 1950; (2) discharge under other than dishonorable conditions; and (3) 181 days continuous active duty service unless discharged early for a service-connected disability.

Korean War: (1) active duty after June 26, 1950, and prior to Feb. 1, 1955; (2) discharge under other than dishonorable conditions; and (3) at least 90 days total service, unless discharged early for a service-connected disability.

Post-Korean War period: (1) active duty after Jan. 31, 1955, and prior to Aug. 5, 1964; (2) discharge under other than dishonorable conditions; (3) 181 days continuous service, unless discharged early for a service-connected disability.

Vietnam War: (1) active duty after Aug. 4, 1964, and prior to May 8, 1975; (2) discharge under other than dishonorable conditions; and (3) 90 days total service, unless discharged early for a service-connected disability. For veterans who served in the Republic of Vietnam, the beginning date is Feb. 28, 1961.

Post-Vietnam period: (1) active duty after May 7, 1975, and prior to Aug. 2, 1990; (2) active duty for 181 continuous days, all of which occurred after May 7, 1975; and (3) discharge under conditions other than dishonorable or early discharge for service-connected disability.

24-Month Rule: If service was between Sept. 8, 1980, (Oct. 16, 1981, for officers) and Aug. 1, 1990, veterans must generally complete 24 months of continuous active duty service or the full period (at least 181 days) for which they were called or ordered to active duty, and be discharged under conditions other than dishonorable.

Exceptions are allowed if the veteran completed at least 181 days of active duty service but was discharged earlier than 24 months for (1) hardship, (2) the convenience of the government, (3) reduction-in-force, (4) certain medical conditions, or (5) service-connected disability.

Gulf War: Veterans of the Gulf War era -- Aug. 2, 1990, to a date to be determined -- must generally complete 24 months of continuous active duty service or the full period (at least 90 days) for which they were called to active duty, and be discharged under other than dishonorable conditions.

Exceptions are allowed if the veteran completed at least 90 days of active duty but was discharged earlier than 24 months for (1) hardship, (2) the convenience of the government, (3) reduction-in-force, (4) certain medical conditions, or (5) service-connected disability. Reservists and National Guard members are eligible if they were activated after Aug. 1, 1990, served at least 90 days, and received an honorable discharge.

Active Duty Personnel: Until the Gulf War era is ended, persons on active duty are eligible after serving 90 continuous days.

VA Guaranty Amount Varies with the size of the loan and the location of the property. Because lenders are able to obtain this guaranty from VA, borrowers do not need to make a down payment, provided they have enough home loan entitlement.

VA will guarantee 25 percent of the principal loan amount, up to the maximum guaranty. The maximum guaranty varies depending upon the location of the property.

For all locations in the United States other than Alaska, Guam, Hawaii, and the U.S. Virgin Islands, the maximum guaranty is the greater of 25 percent of (a) $417,000 or (b) 125 percent of the area median price for a single-family residence, but in no case will the guaranty exceed 175 percent of the Freddie Mac loan limit for a single-family residence in the county in which the property securing the loan is located. This translates to a maximum loan amount of $1,094,625 for 2010.

In Alaska, Guam, Hawaii, and the U.S. Virgin Islands, the maximum guaranty is the greater of 25 percent of (a) $625,500 or (b) 125 percent of the area median price for a single-family residence, but in no case will the guaranty exceed 175 percent of the Freddie Mac loan

limit for a single-family residence in the county in which the property securing the loan is located. This translates to a maximum loan
amount of $1,641,937.50 for 2010.

A list of 2010 county loan limits can be found at the following Web
site: www.homeloans.va.gov/loan_limits.htmf

The VA funding fee and up to $6,000 of energy-efficient improve-
ments can be included in VA loans. Other closing costs must be paid
by the veteran, except on refinancing loans where most costs can be
included in the loan.

Loan Amount	Maximum Guaranty	Special Provisions
Up to $45,000	50% of loan amount	25% on Interest Rate Reduction Refinancing Loans
$45,001 - $56,250	$22,500	Same as above
$56,251 - $144,000	40% of the loan amount, with a maximum of $36,000	Same as above
$144,000 or more	Up to an amount equal to 25% of the county loan limit	Same as above

An eligible borrower can use a VA-guaranteed Interest Rate Reduction Refinancing Loan to refinance an existing VA loan to lower the
interest rate and payment. Typically, no credit underwriting is required for this type of loan. The loan may include the entire outstanding balance of the prior loan, the costs of energy-efficient improvements, as well as closing costs, including up to two discount points.

An eligible borrower who wishes to obtain a VA-guaranteed loan to
purchase a manufactured home or lot can borrow up to 95 percent
of the home's purchase price. The amount VA will guarantee on a
manufactured home loan is 40 percent of the loan amount or the
veteran's available entitlement, up to a maximum amount of $20,000.

VA Appraisals: No loan can be guaranteed by VA without first being
appraised by a VA-assigned fee appraiser. A lender can request a VA
appraisal by accessing The Appraisal System (TAS), which is located

in the VA Veteran Information Portal (VIP). TAS electronically assigns appraisals to VA Fee Appraisers on a rotational basis. The requester pays for the appraisal upon completion, according to a fee schedule approved by VA. This VA appraisal estimates the value of the property. It is not an inspection and does not guarantee the house is free of defects. VA guarantees the loan, not the condition of the property.

Closing Costs: For purchase home loans, payment in cash is required on all closing costs, including title search and recording fees, hazard insurance premiums and prepaid taxes. For refinancing loans, all such costs may be included in the loan, as long as the total loan does not exceed the reasonable value of the property. Interest rate reduction loans may include closing costs, including a maximum of two discount points.

All veterans, except those receiving VA disability compensation, those who are rated by VA as eligible to receive compensation as a result of pre-discharge disability examination and rating, and unmarried surviving spouses of veterans who died in service or as a result of a service-connected disability, are charged a VA funding fee. For all types of loans, the loan amount may include this funding fee.

Required Occupancy: To qualify for a VA home loan, a veteran or the spouse of an active duty servicemember must certify that he or she intends to occupy the home. When refinancing a VA-guaranteed loan solely to reduce the interest rate, a veteran need only certify to prior occupancy.

Financing, Interest Rates and Terms: Veterans obtain VA-guaranteed loans through the usual lending institutions, including banks, credit unions, and mortgage brokers. VA-guaranteed loans can have either a fixed interest rate or an adjustable rate, where the interest rate may adjust up to one percent annually and up to five percent over the life of the loan. VA does not set the interest rate. Interest rates are negotiable between the lender and borrower on all loan types.

Veterans may also choose a different type of adjustable rate mortgage called a hybrid ARM, where the initial interest rate remains fixed for three to 10 years. If the rate remains fixed for less than five years, the rate adjustment cannot be more than one percent annually and five percent over the life of the loan. For a hybrid ARM with an initial fixed period of five years or more, the initial adjustment may be up to two percent. The Secretary has the authority to determine annual adjustments thereafter. Currently annual adjustments may be up to two percentage points and six percent over the life of the loan.

If the lender charges discount points on the loan, the veteran may negotiate with the seller as to who will pay points or if they will be split between buyer and seller. Points paid by the veteran may not be included in the loan (with the exception that up to two points may be included in interest rate reduction refinancing loans). The term of the loan may be for as long as 30 years and 32 days.

Loan Assumption Requirements and Liability: VA loans made on or after March 1, 1988, are not assumable without the prior approval of VA or its authorized agent (usually the lender collecting the monthly payments). To approve the assumption, the lender must ensure that the borrower is a satisfactory credit risk and will assume all of the veteran's liabilities on the loan. If approved, the borrower will have to pay a funding fee that the lender sends to VA, and the veteran will be released from liability to the federal government. A release of liability does not mean that a veteran's guaranty entitlement is restored. That occurs only if the borrower is an eligible veteran who agrees to substitute his or her entitlement for that of the seller. If a veteran allows assumption of a loan without prior approval, then the lender may demand immediate and full payment of the loan, and the veteran may be liable if the loan is foreclosed and VA has to pay a claim under the loan guaranty.

Loans made prior to March 1, 1988, are generally freely assumable, but veterans should still request VA's approval in order to be released of liability. Veterans whose loans were closed after Dec. 31, 1989, usually have no liability to the government following a foreclosure, except in cases involving fraud, misrepresentation, or bad faith, such as allowing an unapproved assumption. However, for the entitlement to be restored, any loss suffered by VA must be paid in full.

2010 VA Funding Fees

A funding fee must be paid to VA unless the veteran is exempt from such a fee because he or she receives VA disability compensation. The fee may be paid in cash or included in the loan. Closing costs such as VA appraisal, credit report, loan processing fee, title search, title insurance, recording fees, transfer taxes, survey charges, or hazard insurance may not be included in the loan.

Loan Category	Active Duty and Veterans	Reservists and National Guard
Loans for purchase or construction with downpayments of less than 5%, refinancing, and home improvement	2.15 percent	2.40 percent
Loans for purchase or construction with downpayments of at least 5% but less than 10%	1.50 percent	1.75 percent
Loans for purchase or construction with downpayments of 10% or more	1.25 percent	1.50 percent
Loans for manufactured homes	1 percent	1 percent
Interest rate reduction refinancing loans	.50 percent	.50 percent
Assumption of a VA-guaranteed loan	.50 percent	.50 percent
Second or subsequent use of entitlement with no downpayment	3.3 percent	3.3 percent

VA Assistance to Veterans in Default: When a veteran's home loan becomes delinquent, the veteran should contact the lender as soon as possible to explain what caused the missed payments, and discuss how they can be repaid. Depending on a veteran's situation, the lender may offer any of the following options to avoid foreclosure:

- **Repayment Plan:** make a regular payment each month plus part of the late payments.
- **Forbearance:** lender temporarily suspends payments to

allow veteran time to accumulate funds to reinstate the loan or sell the property.

- **Loan Modification:** lender provides a fresh start by adding delinquency to the loan balance, and establishing a new payment schedule.
- **Compromise Sale/Short Sale:** lender approves a sale of the home for less than what is needed to pay off the loan. The remainder is written off and/or paid by VA guaranty.
- **Deed-in-Lieu-of Foreclosure:** lender accepts a deed to the property instead of going through a lengthy foreclosure process.

VA does not have funds to lend veterans to make delinquent payments, but can offer financial counseling to veterans with VA-guaranteed, conventional, or sub-prime loans. For veterans with VA-guaranteed loans, VA may be able to intercede with the lender to help arrange an alternative option to foreclosure, but does not have that authority on other loans. VA's toll-free number for the Home Loan Guaranty program is 1-877-827-3702.

VA Acquires Property Foreclosures

VA acquires properties as a result of foreclosures. A private contractor is currently marketing the properties through listing agents using local Multiple Listing Services. A listing of "VA Properties for Sale" may be found at va.reotrans.com. Contact a real estate agent for information on purchasing a VA-acquired property.

Loans for Native American Veterans

Eligible Native American veterans can obtain a loan from VA to purchase, construct, or improve a home on Federal Trust Land, or to reduce the interest rate on such a VA loan. Native American Direct Loans are only available if a memorandum of understanding exists between the tribal organization and VA.

Veterans who are not Native American, but who are married to Native American non-veterans, may be eligible for a direct loan under this program. To be eligible for such a loan, the qualified non-Native American veteran and the Native American spouse must reside on Federal Trust Land, and both the veteran and spouse must have a meaningful interest in the dwelling or lot.

The following safeguards have been established to protect veterans:

1. VA may suspend from the loan program those who take unfair advantage of veterans or discriminate because of race, color, religion, sex, disability, family status, or national origin.
2. The builder of a new home (or manufactured) is required to give the purchasing veteran either a one-year warranty or a 10-year insurance-backed protection plan.
3. The borrower obtaining a loan may only be charged closing costs allowed by VA.
4. The borrower can prepay without penalty the entire loan or any part not less than one installment or $100.
5. VA encourages holders to extend forbearance if a borrower becomes temporarily unable to meet the terms of the loan.

Chapter 6

VA Life Insurance

For complete details on government life insurance, visit the VA Internet site at www.insurance.va.gov/ or call VA's Insurance Center toll-free at 1-800-669-8477. Specialists are available between the hours of 8:30 a.m. and 6 p.m., Eastern Time, to discuss premium payments, insurance dividends, address changes, policy loans, naming beneficiaries and reporting the death of the insured.

If the insurance policy number is not known, send whatever information is available, such as the veteran's VA file number, date of birth, Social Security number, military serial number or military service branch and dates of service to:

Department of Veterans Affairs
Regional Office and Insurance Center
Box 42954
Philadelphia, PA 19101

For information about Servicemembers' Group Life Insurance, Veterans Group Life Insurance, Servicemembers' Group Life Insurance Traumatic Injury Protection, or Servicemembers' Group Life Insurance Family Coverage, visit the Web site above or call the Office of Servicemembers' Group Life Insurance directly at 1-800-419-1473.

Servicemembers' Group Life Insurance
The following are automatically insured for $400,000 under Service members' Group Life Insurance (SGLI):
   1. Active-duty members of the Army, Navy, Air Force, Marines and Coast Guard.
   2. Commissioned members of the National Oceanic and Atmospheric Administration (NOAA) and the Public Health Service (PHS).
   3. Cadets or midshipmen of the U.S. military academies.
   4. Members, cadets and midshipmen of the ROTC while engaged in authorized training and practice cruises.
   5. Members of the Ready Reserves/National Guard who are

scheduled to perform at least 12 periods of inactive training per year.

6. Members who volunteer for a mobilization category in the Individual Ready Reserve.

Individuals may elect in writing to be covered for a lesser amount or not at all. Part-time coverage may be provided to reservists who do not qualify for full-time coverage. Premiums are automatically deducted from the service member's pay. At the time of separation from service, SGLI can be converted to either Veterans' Group Life Insurance (VGLI) or a commercial plan through participating companies. SGLI coverage continues for 120 days after separation at no charge. Coverage of $10,000 is also automatically provided for dependent children of members insured under SGLI with no premium required.

SGLI Traumatic Injury Protection

Members of the armed services serve our nation heroically during times of great need, but what happens when they experience great needs of their own because they have sustained a traumatic injury? Servicemembers' Group Life Insurance Traumatic Injury Protection (TSGLI) helps severely injured service members through their time of need with a one-time payment. The amount varies depending on the injury, but it could make a difference in the lives of service members by allowing their families to be with them during their recovery. TSGLI helps them with unforeseen expenses; or gives them a financial head start on life after recovery.

TSGLI is an insurance program that is bundled with Servicemembers' Group Life Insurance (SGLI). An additional $1.00 has been added to the service member's SGLI premium to cover TSGLI. After Dec. 1, 2005, all service members who are covered by SGLI are automatically also covered by TSGLI, regardless of where their qualifying traumatic injury occurred. However, TSGLI claims require approval.

In addition, there is retroactive TSGLI coverage for service members who sustained a qualifying traumatic injury while in theater supporting Operation Enduring Freedom (OEF), Operation Iraqi Freedom (OIF), or while on orders in a Combat Zone Tax Exclusion (CZTE) area from Oct. 7, 2001, through Nov. 30, 2005. TSGLI coverage is available for these service members regardless of whether SGLI coverage was in force.

For more information, and branch of service contact information, visit the Web site at www.insurance.va.gov/sgliSite/TSGLI/TSGLI. htm, or call 1-800-237-1336 (Army); 1-800-368-3202 (Navy); 1-877-216-0825 (Marine Corps); 1-800-433-0048 (Active Duty Air Force); 1-800-525-0102 (Air Force Reserves); 1-703-607-0901 (Air National Guard); 1-202-475-5391 (U.S. Coast Guard); 1-301-594-2963 (PHS); or 1-301-713-3444 (NOAA).

Servicemembers' Group Life Insurance Family Coverage

Servicemembers' Group Life Insurance Family Coverage (FSGLI) provides up to $100,000 of life insurance coverage for spouses of service members with full-time SGLI coverage, not to exceed the amount of SGLI the member has in force. FSGLI is a service members' benefit; the member pays the premium and is the only person allowed to be the beneficiary of the coverage. FSGLI spousal coverage ends when: 1) the service member elects in writing to terminate coverage on the spouse; 2) the service member elects to terminate his or her own SGLI coverage; 3) the service member dies; 4) the service member separates from service; or 5) the service member divorces the spouse. The insured spouse may convert his or her FSGLI coverage to a policy offered by participating private insurers within 120 days of the date of any of the termination events noted above.

Veterans' Group Life Insurance

SGLI may be converted to Veterans' Group Life Insurance (VGLI), which provides renewable term coverage to:

1. Veterans who had full-time SGLI coverage upon release from active duty or the reserves.
2. Members of the Ready Reserves/National Guard with part-time SGLI coverage who incur a disability or aggravate a pre-existing disability during a period of active duty or a period of inactive duty for less than 31 days that renders them uninsurable at standard premium rates.
3. Members of the Individual Ready Reserve and Inactive National Guard.

SGLI can be converted to VGLI up to the amount of coverage the service member had when separated from service. Veterans who submit an application and the initial premium within 120 days of leaving the service will be covered regardless of their health. Veterans who don't apply within this period can still convert to VGLI if they submit an application, pay the initial premium, and show evidence of insurability within one year after the end of the 120 day period.

SGLI Disability Extension

Servicemembers who are totally disabled at the time of separation are eligible for free SGLI Disability Extension of up to two years. They must apply to the Office of Servicemembers' Group Life Insurance (OSGLI) at 80 Livingston Ave., Roseland, New Jersey 07068-1733.

Those covered under the SGLI Disability Extension are automatically converted to VGLI at the end of their extension period. VGLI is convertible at any time to a permanent plan policy with any participating commercial insurance company.

Accelerated Death Benefits

SGLI, FSGLI and VGLI policyholders who are terminally ill (prognosis of nine months or less to live) have a one-time option of requesting up to 50 percent of their coverage amount paid in advance.

Service-Disabled Veterans' Insurance

A veteran who was discharged under other than dishonorable conditions and who has a service-connected disability but is otherwise in good health may apply to VA for up to $10,000 in life insurance coverage under the Service-Disabled Veterans' Insurance (S-DVI) program. Applications must be submitted within two years from the date of being notified of the approval of a new service-connected disability by VA. This insurance is limited to veterans who left service on or after April 25, 1951.

Veterans who are totally disabled may apply for a waiver of premiums and additional supplemental insurance coverage of up to $20,000. However, premiums cannot be waived on the additional supplemental insurance. To be eligible for this type of supplemental insurance, veterans must meet all of the following three requirements:

1. Be under age 65.
2. Be eligible for a waiver of premiums due to total disability.
3. Apply for additional insurance within one year from the date of notification of waiver approval on the S-DVI policy.

Veterans' Mortgage Life Insurance

Veterans' Mortgage Life Insurance (VMLI) is mortgage protection insurance available to severely disabled veterans who have been approved by VA for a Specially Adapted Housing Grant (SAH). Maximum coverage is the amount of the existing mortgage up to $90,000, and is payable only to the mortgage company. Protection is issued automatically following SAH approval, provided the veteran submits information required to establish a premium and does not decline coverage. Coverage automatically terminates when the mortgage is paid off. If a mortgage is disposed of through sale of the property, VMLI may be obtained on the mortgage of another home.

Other Insurance Information

The following information applies to policies issued to World War I, World War II, Korean, and Vietnam-era veterans and any Service-Disabled Veterans Insurance policies. Policies in this group are prefixed by the letters K, V, RS, W, J, JR, JS, or RH.

Insurance Dividends Issued Annually: World War I, World War II, and Korean-era veterans with active policies beginning with the letters V, RS, W, J, JR, JS, or K are issued tax-free dividends annually on the policy anniversary date. (Policies prefixed by RH do not earn dividends.) Policyholders do not need to apply for dividends, but may select from among the following dividend options:

1. Cash: The dividend is paid directly to the insured either by a mailed check or by direct deposit to a bank account.
2. Paid-Up Additional Insurance: The dividend is used to purchase additional insurance coverage.
3. Credit or Deposit: The dividend is held in an account for the policyholder with interest. Withdrawals from the account can be made at any time. The interest rate may be adjusted.
4. Net Premium Billing Options: These options use the dividend to pay the annual policy premium. If the dividend exceeds the premium, the policyholder has options to choose how the remainder is used. If the dividend is not enough to pay an annual premium, the policyholder is billed the balance.
5. Other Dividend Options: Dividends can also be used to repay a loan or pay premiums in advance.

Reinstating Lapsed Insurance: Lapsed term policies may be reinstated within five years from the date of lapse. A five-year term policy that is not lapsed at the end of the term is automatically renewed for an additional five years. Lapsed permanent plans may be reinstated within certain time limits and with certain health requirements. Reinstated permanent plan policies require repayment of all back premiums, plus interest.

Converting Term Policies: Term policies are renewed automatically every five years, with premiums increasing at each renewal. Premiums do not increase after age 70. Term policies may be converted to permanent plans, which have fixed premiums for life and earn cash and loan values.

Paid-up Insurance Available on Term Policies: Effective September 2000, VA provides paid-up insurance on term policies whose premiums have been capped. Veterans with National Service Life Insurance (NSLI) term insurance that has renewed at age 71 or older and who stop paying premiums on their policies will be given a termination dividend. This dividend will be used to purchase a reduced amount of paid-up insurance, which insures the veteran for life with no premium payments required. The amount of insurance remains level. This does not apply to S-DVI (RH) policies.

Borrowing on Policies: Policyholders with permanent plan policies may borrow up to 94 percent of the cash surrender value of their insurance after the insurance is in force for one year or more. Interest is compounded annually. The loan interest rate is variable and may be obtained by calling toll-free 1-800-669-8477.

Chapter 7

Burial and Memorial Benefits

Eligibility

Veterans discharged from active duty under conditions other than dishonorable and service members who die while on active duty, active duty for training, or inactive duty training, as well as spouses and dependent children of Veterans and active duty servicemembers, may be eligible for VA burial and memorial benefits. The Veteran does not have to die before a spouse or dependent child for them to be eligible.

With certain exceptions, active duty service beginning after Sept. 7, 1980, as an enlisted person, and after Oct. 16, 1981, as an officer, must be for a minimum of 24 consecutive months or the full period of active duty (as in the case of reservists or National Guard members called to active duty for a limited duration). Active duty for training, by itself, while serving in the reserves or National Guard, is not sufficient to confer eligibility. Reservists and National Guard members, as well as their spouses and dependent children, are eligible if they were entitled to retired pay at the time of death, or would have been upon reaching requisite age. See Chapter 8 for more information.

VA's National Cemetery Scheduling Office or local national cemetery directors verify eligibility for burial. A copy of the Veteran's discharge document that specifies the period(s) of active duty and character of discharge is usually sufficient to determine eligibility. In some instances, a copy of the deceased's death certificate and proof of relationship to the Veteran (for eligible family members) may be required.

Under Section 2411 of Title 38 of the United States Code, certain otherwise eligible individuals found to have committed federal or state capital crimes are barred from burial or memorialization in a VA national cemetery, and from receipt of government-furnished headstones, markers, burial flags, and Presidential Memorial Certificates.

Veterans and other claimants for VA burial benefits have the right to appeal decisions made by VA regarding eligibility for national cemetery burial or other memorial benefits. Chapter 13 discusses the procedures for appealing VA claims.

This chapter contains information on the full range of VA burial and memorial benefits. Readers with questions may contact the nearest national cemetery, listed by state in the VA Facilities section of this book, call 1-800-827-1000, or visit the Web site at www.cem.va.gov/.

Burial in VA National Cemeteries

Burial in a VA national cemetery is available for eligible Veterans, their spouses and dependents at no cost to the family and includes the gravesite, grave-liner, opening and closing of the grave, a headstone or marker, and perpetual care as part of a national shrine. For Veterans, benefits also include a burial flag (with case for active duty) and military funeral honors. Family members and other loved ones of deceased Veterans may request Presidential Memorial Certificates.

VA operates 131 national cemeteries, of which 71 are open for new casketed interments and 19 are open to accept only cremated remains. Burial options are limited to those available at a specific cemetery but may include in-ground casket, or interment of cremated remains in a columbarium, in ground or in a scatter garden. Contact the national cemetery directly, or visit our Web site at: www.cem. va.gov/ to determine if a particular cemetery is open for new burials, and which other options are available.

The funeral director or the next of kin makes interment arrangements by contacting the National Cemetery Scheduling Office or national cemetery in which burial is desired. VA normally does not conduct burials on weekends. Gravesites cannot be reserved; however, VA will honor reservations made under previous programs.

Surviving spouses of Veterans who died on or after Jan. 1, 2000, do not lose eligibility for burial in a national cemetery if they remarry. Burial of dependent children is limited to unmarried children under 21 years of age, or under 23 years of age if a full-time student at an approved educational institution. Unmarried adult children who become physically or mentally disabled and incapable of self-support before age 21, or age 23 if a full-time student, also are eligible for burial.

Headstones and Markers: Veterans, active duty service members, and retired Reservists and National Guard service members, are eligible for an inscribed headstone or marker for their grave at any cemetery – national, State Veterans, or private. VA will deliver a headstone or marker at no cost, anywhere in the world. For eligible Veterans whose deaths occurred on or after Nov. 1, 1990, VA may provide a government headstone or marker even if the grave is already marked with a private one. Spouses and dependent children are eligible for a government headstone or marker only if they are buried in a national or State Veterans cemetery.

Flat markers are available in bronze, granite or marble. Upright headstones come in granite or marble. In national cemeteries, the style chosen will be consistent with existing monuments at the place of burial. Niche markers are available to mark columbaria used for inurnment of cremated remains.

Headstones and markers previously provided by the government may be replaced at the government's expense if badly deteriorated, illegible, vandalized or stolen. To check the status of a claim for a headstone or marker for a national or State Veterans cemetery, call the cemetery. To check the status of one being placed in a private cemetery, call 1-800-697-6947.

Inscription: Headstones and markers must be inscribed with the name of the deceased, branch of service, and year of birth and death. They also may be inscribed with other optional information, including an authorized emblem of belief and, space permitting, additional text including military rank; war service such as "World War II;" complete dates of birth and death; military awards; military organizations; civilian or Veteran affiliations; and personalized words of endearment.

Private Cemeteries: To submit a claim for a headstone or marker for a private cemetery, mail a completed VA Form 40-1330 (available at www4.va.gov/vaforms/va/pdf/VA40-1330.pdf), Application for Standard Government Headstone or Marker, and a copy of the Veteran's military discharge document to Memorial Programs Service (41A1), Department of Veterans Affairs, 5109 Russell Rd., Quantico, VA 22134-3903. The form and supporting documents may also be faxed toll free to 1-800-455-7143.

Before ordering, check with the cemetery to ensure that the Government-furnished headstone or marker will be accepted. All installation fees are the responsibility of the applicant.

"In Memory Of" Markers: VA provides memorial headstones and markers with "In Memory Of" as the first line of inscription, to memorialize those whose remains have not been recovered or identified, were buried at sea, donated to science or cremated and scattered. Eligibility is the same as for regular headstones and markers. There is no fee when the "In Memory Of" marker is placed in a national cemetery. All installation fees are the responsibility of the applicant.

Medallions in Lieu of Government Headstone/Marker: Public Law 110-157 enacted December 26, 2007, expanded VA authority to provide a medallion instead of a headstone or marker for Veterans' graves in private cemeteries when the grave is already marked with a privately-purchased headstone or marker. Claimants will have the option to apply for either a traditional headstone or marker to place on the grave, or a medallion to affix to a privately-purchased headstone or marker. VA anticipates the medallion will be available during 2010. Current information regarding medallion availability is located at www.cem.va.gov.

Presidential Memorial Certificates are issued upon request to recognize the United States military service of honorably discharged deceased Veterans. Next of kin, relatives and other loved ones may apply for a certificate by mailing, e-mailing, or faxing a completed and signed VA Form 40-0247 along with a copy of the Veteran's military discharge documents or proof of honorable military service. The form and eligibility requirements can be found at www.cem.va.gov. All requests must be sent with supporting military documents or proof of honorable military service.

Completed and signed documents along with supporting military documents can be submitted as follows:
- By US Mail to the Department of Veterans Affairs, Presidential Memorial Certificates Program (41A1C), 5109 Russell Road, Quantico VA 22134.
- Faxed to our toll free fax service at 1-800-455-7143.
- Scanned and attached to an e-mail addressed to: pmc@ va.gov. E-mail requests must have forms and documents attached.

For all PMC requests for deceased active duty service members, we encourage you to send documents to the Washington, DC fax line at 1-202-565-8054. Please be sure to provide a copy of the service member's DD Form 1300 (Report of Casualty) with each request.

Burial Flags: VA will furnish a U.S. burial flag to memorialize:
1. Veterans who served during wartime or after Jan. 31, 1955.
2. Veterans who were entitled to retired pay for service in the Reserve or National Guard, or would have been entitled if over age 60.
3. Members or former members of the Selected Reserve who served their initial obligation, or were discharged for a disability incurred or aggravated in the line of duty, or died while a member of the Selected Reserve.

Reimbursement of Burial Expenses: VA will pay a burial allowance up to $2,000 if the Veteran's death is service-connected. In such cases, the person who bore the Veteran's burial expenses may claim reimbursement from VA.

In some cases, VA will pay the cost of transporting the remains of a Veteran whose death was service-connected to the nearest national cemetery with available gravesites. There is no time limit for filing reimbursement claims in service-connected death cases.

Burial Allowance: VA will pay a $300 burial and funeral allowance for Veterans who, at time of death, were entitled to receive pension or compensation or would have been entitled if they were not receiving military retirement pay. Eligibility also may be established when death occurs in a VA facility, a VA-contracted nursing home or a State Veterans nursing home. In cases in which the Veteran's death was not service-connected, claims must be filed within two years after burial or cremation.

Plot Allowance: VA will pay a $300 plot allowance when a Veteran is buried in a cemetery not under U.S. government jurisdiction if: the Veteran was discharged from active duty because of disability incurred or aggravated in the line of duty; the Veteran was receiving compensation or pension or would have been if the Veteran was not receiving military retired pay; or the Veteran died in a VA facility.

The $300 plot allowance may be paid to the state for the cost of a plot or interment in a state-owned cemetery reserved solely for Veteran burials if the Veteran is buried without charge. Burial expenses paid by the deceased's employer or a state agency will not be reimbursed.

Military Funeral Honors: Upon request, DoD will provide military funeral honors consisting of folding and presentation of the United States flag and the playing of "Taps." A funeral honors detail consists of two or more uniformed members of the armed forces, with at least one member from the deceased's branch of service.

Family members should inform their funeral director if they want military funeral honors. DoD maintains a toll-free number (1-877-MIL-HONR) for use by funeral directors only to request honors. VA can help arrange honors for burials at VA national cemeteries. Veterans service organizations or volunteer groups may help provide honors. For more information, visit www.militaryfuneralhonors.osd.mil/.

Veterans Cemeteries Administered by Other Agencies

Arlington National Cemetery: Administered by the Department of the Army. Eligibility is more restrictive than at VA national cemeteries. For information, call (703) 607-8000, write Superintendent, Arlington National Cemetery, Arlington, VA 22211, or visit www.arlingtoncemetery.org/.

Department of the Interior: Administers two active national cemeteries – Andersonville National Cemetery in Georgia and Andrew Johnson National Cemetery in Tennessee. Eligibility is similar to VA national cemeteries.

State Veterans Cemeteries: Seventy-four State Veterans cemeteries offer burial options for Veterans and their families. These cemeteries have similar eligibility requirements but many require state residency. Some services, particularly for family members, may require a fee. Contact the State cemetery or State Veterans affairs office for information. To locate a State Veterans cemetery, visit www. cem.va.gov/cem/scg/lsvc.asp.

Chapter 8
Reserve and National Guard

Eligibility for VA Benefits

Reservists who serve on active duty establish veteran status and may be eligible for the full-range of VA benefits, depending on the length of active military service and a discharge or release from active duty under conditions other than dishonorable. In addition, reservists not activated may qualify for some VA benefits.

National Guard members can establish eligibility for VA benefits if activated for federal service during a period of war or domestic emergency. Activation for other than federal service does not qualify guard members for all VA benefits. Claims for VA benefits based on federal service filed by members of the National Guard should include a copy of the military orders, presidential proclamation or executive order that clearly demonstrates the federal nature of the service.

Qualifying for VA Health Care

Effective Jan. 28, 2008, veterans discharged from active duty on or after Jan. 28, 2003, are eligible for enhanced enrollment placement into Priority Group 6 (unless eligible for higher Priority Group placement) for 5 years post discharge. Veterans with combat service after Nov. 11, 1998, who were discharged from active duty before Jan. 28, 2003, and who apply for enrollment on or after Jan. 28, 2008, are eligible for this enhanced enrollment benefit through Jan. 27, 2011.

Activated reservists and members of the National Guard are eligible if they served on active duty in a theater of combat operations after Nov. 11, 1998, and, have been discharged under other than dishonorable conditions.

Veterans who enroll with VA under this "Combat Veteran" authority will retain enrollment eligibility even after their five-year post discharge period ends. At the end of their post discharge period, VA will reassess the veteran's information (including all applicable eligibility factors) and make a new enrollment decision. For additional information, call 1-877-222-VETS (8387).

Disability Benefits

VA pays monthly compensation benefits for disabilities incurred or aggravated during active duty and active duty for training as a result of injury or disease, and for disabilities due to injury, heart attack, or stroke that occurred during inactive duty training. For additional information see Chapter 2, "Veterans with Service-Connected Disabilities".

Montgomery GI Bill – Selected Reserve

Members of reserve elements of the Army, Navy, Air Force, Marine Corps and Coast Guard, and members of the Army National Guard and the Air National Guard, may be entitled to up to 36 months of educational benefits under the Montgomery GI Bill (MGIB) – Selected Reserve. To be eligible, the participant must:

1. Have a six-year obligation in the Selected Reserve or National Guard signed after June 30, 1985, or, if an officer, agree to serve six years in addition to the original obligation.
2. Complete initial active duty for training.
3. Have a high school diploma or equivalency certificate before applying for benefits.
4. Remain in good standing in a Selected Reserve or National Guard unit.

Reserve components determine eligibility for benefits. VA does not make decisions about eligibility and cannot make payments until the reserve component has determined eligibility and notified VA.

Period of Eligibility: Benefits generally end the day a reservist or National Guard member separates from the military. Additionally, if in the Selected Reserve and called to active duty, VA can generally extend the eligibility period by the length of time on active duty plus four months for each period of active duty. Once this extension is granted, it will not be taken away if you leave the Selected Reserve.

Eligible members separated because of unit deactivation, a disability that was not caused by misconduct, or otherwise involuntarily separated during Oct. 1, 1991, through Dec. 31, 2001, have 14 years after their eligibility date to use benefits. Similarly, members involuntarily separated from the Selected Reserve due to a deactivation of their unit between Oct. 1, 2007, and Sept. 30, 2014, may receive a 14-year period of eligibility.

Payments: The rate for full-time training effective Oct. 1, 2009, is $333 a month for 36 months. Part-time benefits are reduced proportionately. For complete current rates, visit www.gibill.va.gov/. DOD may make additional contributions.

Training: Participants may pursue training at a college or university, or take technical training at any approved facility. Training includes undergraduate, graduate, or post-graduate courses; State licensure and certification; courses for a certificate or diploma from business, technical or vocational schools; cooperative training; apprenticeship or on-the-job training; correspondence courses; independent study programs; flight training; entrepreneurship training; or remedial, deficiency or refresher courses needed to complete a program of study.

Accelerated payments for certain high-cost programs are authorized effective Jan. 28, 2008.

Work-Study: Participants who train at the three-quarter or full-time rate may be eligible for a work-study program in which they work for VA and receive hourly wages. Students under the work-study program must be supervised by a VA employee and all duties performed must relate to VA. The types of work allowed include:
1. VA paperwork processing at schools or other training facilities.
2. Assistance with patient care at VA hospitals or domiciliary care facilities.
3. Work at national or state veterans' cemeteries.
4. Various jobs within any VA regional office.
5. Other VA-approved activities.

*MGIB – Selected Reserve work-study students may also assist with an activity relating to the administration of this education benefit at DOD, Coast Guard, or National Guard facilities.

Educational and Vocational Counseling: Refer to Chapter 10, "Transition Assistance", for detailed information on available services.

Reserve Educational Assistance Program (REAP)
This program provides educational assistance to members of National Guard and reserve components – Selected Reserve and Individual Ready Reserve (IRR) – who are called or ordered to active duty service in response to a war or national emergency as declared by the

President or Congress. Visit www.gibill.va.gov/ for more information.

Eligibility: Eligibility is determined by DOD or the Department of Homeland Security. Generally, a servicemember who serves on active duty on or after Sept.11, 2001, for at least 90 consecutive days or accumulates a total of three or more of years of service is eligible.

Payments: Reserve or National Guard members whose eligibility is based upon continuous service receive a payment rate based upon their number of continuous days on active duty. Members who qualify after the accumulation of three or more years aggregate active duty service receive the full payment allowable.

Reserve Educational Assistance Rates

Active Duty, Reserves and National Guard members	Monthly Payment Rate for Full-Time Students
90 days but less than one year	$547.20
One year but less than two years	$820.80
Two or more continuous years	$1,094.40

* Effective Oct. 1, 2009

Training: Participants may pursue training at a college or university, or take technical training at any approved facility. Training includes undergraduate, graduate, or post-graduate courses; state licensure and certification courses; courses for a certificate or diploma from business, technical or vocational schools; cooperative training; apprenticeship or on-the-job training; correspondence courses; independent study programs; flight training; entrepreneurship training; or remedial, deficiency, or refresher courses needed to complete a program of study. Accelerated payments for certain high-cost programs are authorized.

Period of Eligibility: Prior to Jan. 28, 2008, members of the Selected Reserve called to active duty were eligible as long as they continued to serve in the Selected Reserve. They lost eligibility if they went into the Inactive Ready Reserve (IRR). Members of the IRR called to active duty were eligible as long as they stayed in the IRR or Selected Reserve.

Effective Jan. 28, 2008, members who are called up from the Selected Reserve, complete their REAP-qualifying period of active duty service, and then return to the Selected Reserve for the remainder of their service contract, have 10 years to use their benefits after separation.

In addition, members who are called up from the IRR or Inactive National Guard (ING), complete their REAP-qualifying period of active duty service, and then enter the Selected Reserve to complete their service contract, have 10 years to use their benefits after separation.

Work-Study Program: Reserve Education Assistance Program students in the work-study program may also assist with an activity relating to the administration of this education benefit at DOD, Coast Guard, or National Guard facilities.

Educational and Vocational Counseling: Refer to Chapter 10, "Transition Assistance", for detailed information on available services.

Home Loan Guaranty

National Guard members and reservists are eligible for a VA home loan if they have completed at least six years of honorable service, are mobilized for active duty service for a period of at least 90 days, or are discharged because of a service-connected disability.

Reservists who do not qualify for VA housing loan benefits may be eligible for loans on favorable terms insured by the Federal Housing Administration (FHA), part of HUD. Additional information can be found in Chapter 5 -- "Home Loan Guaranty."

Life Insurance

National Guard members and reservists are eligible to receive Servicemembers' Group Life Insurance (SGLI), Veterans' Group Life Insurance (VGLI), and Family Servicemembers' Group Life Insurance (FSGLI). They may also be eligible for SGLI Traumatic Injury Protection if severely injured and suffering a qualifying loss, Service-Disabled Veterans Insurance if they receive a service-connected disability rating from VA, and Veterans' Mortgage Life Insurance if approved for a Specially Adapted Housing Grant.

Complete details can be found in Chapter 6 -- "VA Life Insurance."

Burial and Memorial Benefits

VA provides a burial flag to memorialize members or former members of the Selected Reserve who served their initial obligation, or were discharged for a disability incurred or aggravated in the line of duty, or died while a member of the Selected Reserve. Information about other benefits that may be available can be found in Chapter 7 – "Burial and Memorial Benefits."

Re-employment Rights

A person who left a civilian job to enter active duty in the armed forces is entitled to return to the job after discharge or release from active duty if they:

1. Gave advance notice of military service to the employer.
2. Did not exceed five years cumulative absence from the civilian job (with some exceptions).
3. Submitted a timely application for re-employment.
4. Did not receive a dishonorable or other punitive discharge.

The law calls for a returning veteran to be placed in the job as if he/she had never left, including benefits based on seniority such as pensions, pay increases and promotions. The law also prohibits discrimination in hiring, promotion or other advantages of employment on the basis of military service. Veterans seeking re-employment should apply, verbally or in writing, to the company's hiring official and keep a record of their application. If problems arise, contact the Department of Labor's Veterans' Employment and Training Service (VETS) in the state of the employer.

Federal employees not properly re-employed may appeal directly to the Merit Systems Protection Board. Non-federal employees may file complaints in U.S. District Court. For information, visit www.dol.gov/vets/programs/userra/main.htm.

Army Reserve Warrior and Family Assistance Center

The Army Reserve Warrior and Family Assistance Center (AR-WFAC) provides Army reserve soldiers, veterans, families, and units with a single source to resolve situations related to medical issues and education on programs available to Army reserve soldiers. The center was established in 2007 to ensure that reservists receive appropriate support under the Army Medical Action Plan. The center provides a sponsor to each Army reserve soldier and family currently assigned to a Warrior Transition Unit, Community Based Health Care Organization, or VA PolyTrauma center. The AR-WFAC also assists Army reserve commands at all echelons with the resolution of medical and other issues and provides education on programs and benefits available to Army reserve soldiers. For information, call 1-866-436-6290 or visit www.arfp.org/wfac.

Transition Assistance Advisors

The Transition Assistance Advisor (TAA) program places a National Guard/VA-trained expert at each National Guard State Joint Forces Headquarters to act as an advocate for Guard members and their families within the state. They also serve as advisors on veterans affairs issues for the Family Programs and Joint Forces Headquarters staffs. TAAs receive annual training by VA experts in health care and benefits for both Department of Defense and Department of Veterans Affairs and help Guard members and their families access care at VA and TRICARE facilities in their state or network.

The TAA works with the State Director of Veterans Affairs and other state coalition partners to integrate the delivery of VA and community services to Guard and Reserve veterans. You can reach your Transition Assistance Advisor (TAA) through your state National Guard Joint Forces Headquarters.

Chapter 9
Special Groups of Veterans

Homeless Veterans

VA's homeless programs constitute the largest integrated network of homeless assistance programs in the country, offering a wide array of services to help veterans recover from homelessness and live as self-sufficiently and independently as possible.

The *VA Health Care for Homeless Veterans (HCHV) Program* provides a gateway to VA and community supportive services for eligible Veterans. Through the HCHV Program, Veterans are provided with case management and residential treatment in the community. The program also conducts outreach to homeless Veterans who are not likely to come to VA facilities on their own.

The **National Call Center for Homeless Veterans** (NCCHV) assists homeless veterans, at-risk Veterans, their families and other interested parties with linkages to appropriate VA and community-based resources. The call center provides trained VA staff members 24 hours a day, seven days a week that assess a caller's needs and connect them to appropriate resources. The call center can be accessed by dialing 1-877-4AID VET (1-877-424-3838).

The **VA Grant and Per Diem (GPD) Program** provides funds to non-profit community agencies providing transitional housing (up to 24 months) and/or offering services to homeless veterans, such as case management, education, crisis intervention, counseling, and services targeted towards specialized populations including homeless women Veterans. The goal of the program is helping homeless Veterans achieve residential stability, increase their skill levels and/or income, and obtain greater self-determination.

The **Housing and Urban Development-Veterans Affairs Supported Housing** (HUD-VASH) Program provides permanent housing and ongoing case management for eligible homeless veterans who would not be able to live independently without the support of case management. This program allows eligible veterans to live in veteran-selected housing units with a "Housing Choice" voucher. These vouchers are portable to support the veteran's choice of housing in communities served by their VA medical facility where case management services can be provided. HUD-VASH services include outreach and case management to ensure integration of services and continuity of care. This program enhances the ability of VA to serve homeless women veterans, and homeless veterans with families.

Through the **Supportive Services for Low-Income Veterans Program**, VA aims to improve very low-income Veteran families' housing stability by providing supportive services to very low-income Veteran families in or transitioning to permanent housing. VA funds community-based organizations to provide eligible Veteran families with outreach, case management and assistance in obtaining VA and other benefits. Grantees may also provide time-limited payments to third parties (e.g., landlords, utility companies, moving companies and licensed child care providers) if these payments help Veterans' families stay in or acquire permanent housing on a sustainable basis.

In **VA's Compensated Work Therapy/Transitional Residence** (CWT/TR) Program, disadvantaged, at-risk, and homeless Veterans live in CWT/TR community-based supervised group homes while working for pay in VA's CWT Program, to learn new job skills, relearn successful work habits, and regain a sense of self-esteem and self-worth.

The **Healthcare for Re-Entry Veterans (HCRV) Program** offers outreach, referrals and short-term case management assistance for incarcerated veterans who may be at risk for homelessness upon their release.

For more information on VA homeless programs and services, Veterans currently enrolled in VA health care can speak with their VA mental health or health care provider. Other Veterans and interested parties can find a complete list of VA health care facilities at www. va.gov, or they can call VA's general information hotline at 1-800-827-1000. If assistance is needed when contacting a VA facility, ask to speak to the Health Care for Homeless Veterans Program or the Mental Health service manager. Information is also available on the VA Homeless program Web-site at www.va.gov/homeless.

Filipino Veterans

World War II era Filipino veterans are eligible for certain VA benefits. Generally, Old Philippine Scouts are eligible for VA benefits in the same manner as U.S. veterans. Commonwealth Army veterans, including certain organized Filipino guerrilla forces and New Philippine Scouts residing in the United States who are citizens or lawfully admitted for permanent residence, are also eligible for VA health care in the United States on the same basis as U.S. veterans.

Certain Commonwealth Army veterans and new Philippine Scouts may be eligible for disability compensation and burial benefits. Other veterans of recognized guerrilla groups also may be eligible for certain VA benefits. Survivors of World War II era Filipino veterans may be eligible for dependency and indemnity compensation. Eligibility and the rates of benefits vary based on the recipient's citizenship and place of residence. Call 1-800-827-1000 for additional information.

VA Benefits for Veterans Living Overseas
VA monetary benefits, including disability compensation, pension, educational benefits, and burial allowances are generally payable overseas. Some programs are restricted. Home loan guaranties are available only in the United States and selected U.S. territories and possessions. Educational benefits are limited to approved, degree-granting programs in institutions of higher learning. Beneficiaries living in foreign countries should contact the nearest American embassy or consulate for help. In Canada, contact an office of Veterans Affairs Canada. For information, visit http://www.vba.va.gov/bln/21/Foreign/index.htm.

World War II Era Merchant Marine Seamen
Certain Merchant Marine seamen who served in World War II may qualify for veterans benefits. When applying for medical care, seamen must present their discharge certificate from the Department of Defense. Call 1-800-827-1000 for help obtaining a certificate.

Allied Veterans Who Served During WWI or WWII
VA may provide medical care to certain veterans of nations allied or associated with the United States during World War I or World War II if authorized and reimbursed by the foreign government. VA also may provide hospitalization, outpatient care and domiciliary care to former members of the armed forces of Czechoslovakia or Poland who fought in World War I or World War II in armed conflict against an enemy of the United States if they have been U.S. citizens for at least 10 years.

World War Service by Particular Groups

A number of groups who provided military-related service to the United States can receive VA benefits. A discharge by the Secretary of Defense is needed to qualify. Service in the following groups has been certified as active military service for benefits purposes:

1. Women Air Force Service Pilots (WASPs).
2. World War I Signal Corps Female Telephone Operators Unit.
3. World War I Engineer Field Clerks.
4. Women's Army Auxiliary Corps (WAAC).
5. Quartermaster Corps female clerical employees serving with the American Expeditionary Forces in World War I.
6. Civilian employees of Pacific naval air bases who actively participated in defense of Wake Island during World War II.
7. Reconstruction aides and dietitians in World War I.
8. Male civilian ferry pilots.
9. Wake Island defenders from Guam.
10. Civilian personnel assigned to OSS secret intelligence.
11. Guam Combat Patrol.
12. Quartermaster Corps members of the Keswick crew on Corregidor during World War II.
13. U.S. civilians who participated in the defense of Bataan.
14. U.S. merchant seamen on block ships in support of Operation Mulberry in the World War II invasion of Normandy.
15. American merchant marines in oceangoing service during World War II.
16. Civilian Navy IFF radar technicians who served in combat areas of the Pacific during World War II.
17. U.S. civilians of the American Field Service who served overseas in World War I.
18. U.S. civilians of the American Field Service who served overseas under U.S. armies and U.S. army groups in World War II.
19. U.S. civilian employees of American Airlines who served overseas in a contract with the Air Transport Command between Dec. 14, 1941, and Aug. 14, 1945.
20. Civilian crewmen of U.S. Coast and Geodetic Survey vessels who served in areas of immediate military hazard while conducting cooperative operations with and for the U.S. armed forces between Dec. 7, 1941, and Aug. 15, 1945 Qualifying vessels are: the Derickson, Explorer, Gilber, Hilgard, E. Lester Jones, Lydonia Patton, Surveyor, Wainwright, Westdahl, Oceanographer, Hydrographer and

Pathfinder.
21. Members of the American Volunteer Group (Flying Tigers) who served between Dec. 7, 1941, and July 18, 1942.
22. U.S. civilian flight crew and aviation ground support employees of United Air Lines who served overseas in a contract with Air Transport Command between Dec. 14, 1941, and Aug.14, 1945.
23. U.S. civilian flight crew, including pursers, and aviation ground support employees of Transcontinental and Western Air, Inc. who served overseas in a contract with the Air Transport Command between Dec. 14, 1941, and Aug. 14, 1945.
24. U.S. civilian flight crew and aviation ground support employees of Consolidated Vultee Aircraft Corp. who served overseas in a contract with Air Transport Command between Dec. 14, 1941, and Aug. 14, 1945.
25. U.S. civilian flight crew and aviation ground support employees of Pan American World Airways and its subsidiaries and affiliates, who served overseas in a contract with the Air Transport Command and Naval Air Transport Service between Dec. 14, 1941, and Aug. 14, 1945.
26. Honorably discharged members of the American Volunteer Guard, Eritrea Service Command, between June 21, 1942, and March 31, 1943.
27. U.S. civilian flight crew and aviation ground support employees of Northwest Airlines who served overseas under the airline's contract with Air Transport Command from Dec. 14, 1941, through Aug. 14, 1945.
28. U.S. civilian female employees of the U.S. Army Nurse Corps who served in the defense of Bataan and Corregidor between Jan. 2, 1942, and Feb. 3, 1945.
29. U.S. flight crew and aviation ground support employees of Northeast Airlines Atlantic Division, who served overseas as a result of Northeast Airlines' contract with the Air Transport Command from Dec. 7, 1941, through Aug. 14, 1945.
30. U.S. civilian flight crew and aviation ground support employees of Braniff Airways, who served overseas in the North Atlantic or under the jurisdiction of the North Atlantic Wing, Air Transport Command, as a result of a contract with the Air Transport Command between Feb. 26, 1945, and Aug. 14, 1945.
31. Chamorro and Carolina former native police who received

military training in the Donnal area of central Saipan and
were placed under command of Lt. Casino of the 6th
Provisional Military Police Battalion to accompany U.S.
Marines on active, combat patrol from Aug. 19, 1945, to
Sept. 2, 1945.
32. The operational Analysis Group of the Office of Scientific Research and Development, Office of Emergency
Management, which served overseas with the U.S. Army
Air Corps from Dec. 7, 1941, through Aug. 15, 1945.
33. Service as a member of the Alaska Territorial Guard during
World War II or any individual who was honorably discharged
under section 8147 of the Department of Defense Appropria-
tions Act of 2001.

Incarcerated Veterans

VA benefits are affected if a beneficiary is convicted of a felony and
imprisoned for more than 60 days. Disability or death pension paid to
an incarcerated beneficiary must be discontinued. Disability compensation paid to an incarcerated veteran rated 20 percent or more
disabled is limited to the 10 percent rate. For a veteran whose disability rating is 10 percent, the payment is reduced to half of the rate
payable to a veteran evaluated as 10 percent disabled.

Any amounts not paid may be apportioned to eligible dependents.
Payments are not reduced for participants in work-release programs,
residing in halfway houses or under community control.

Failure to notify VA of a veteran's incarceration can result in overpayment of benefits and the subsequent loss of all VA financial benefits
until the overpayment is recovered. VA benefits will not be provided
to any veteran or dependent wanted for an outstanding felony warrant.

The Healthcare for Reentry Veterans Program (HCRV) offers outreach to veterans incarcerated in state and federal prisons, and
referrals and short-term case management assistance upon release
from prison. The Veterans Justice Outreach Program (VJO) offers
outreach and case management to veterans involved in law enforce-
ment encounters, overseen by treatment courts, and incarcerated in
local jails. Visit www.va.gov/homeless/ to locate an outreach worker.

Chapter 10
Transition Assistance

Joint Transition Assistance

The Departments of Veterans Affairs, Defense, and Labor re-launched a new and improved Web site for wounded warriors – the National Resource Directory (NRD). This directory (www.nationalresourcedirectory.gov) provides access to thousands of services and resources at the national, state and local levels to support recovery, rehabilitation and community reintegration. The NRD is a comprehensive online tool available nationwide for wounded, ill and injured servicemembers, Veterans and their families.

The NRD includes extensive information for Veterans seeking resources on VA benefits, including disability benefits, pensions for Veterans and their families, VA health care insurance and the GI Bill. The NRD's design and interface is simple, easy-to-navigate and intended to answer the needs of a broad audience of users within the military, Veteran and caregiver communities.

Transition From Military to VA

VA has stationed personnel at major military hospitals to help seriously injured servicemembers returning from Operations Enduring Freedom and Iraqi Freedom (OEF/OIF) as they transition from military to civilian life. OEF/OIF servicemembers who have questions about VA benefits or need assistance in filing a VA claim or accessing services can contact the nearest VA office or call 1-800-827-1000.

Transition Assistance Program

The Transition Assistance Program (TAP) consists of comprehensive three-day workshops at military installations designed to help servicemembers as they transition from military to civilian life. The program includes job search, employment and training information, as well as VA benefits information, for servicemembers who are within 12 months of separation or 24 months of retirement. A companion workshop, the Disabled Transition Assistance Program, provides information on VA's Vocational Rehabilitation and Employment Program, as well as other programs for the disabled. Additional information about these programs is available at www.dol.gov/vets/programs/tap/tap_fs.htm.

Pre-Discharge Program

The Pre-Discharge Program is a joint VA and DoD program that affords servicemembers the opportunity to file claims for disability compensation and other benefits up to 180 days prior to separation or retirement.

The two primary components of the Pre-Discharge Program, Benefits Delivery at Discharge (BDD) and Quick Start, may be utilized by all separating CONUS servicemembers on active duty, including members of the Coast Guard, and members of the National Guard and Reserves (activated under Titles 10 or 32).

BDD is offered to accelerate receipt of VA disability benefits, with a goal of providing benefits within 60 days after release or discharge from active duty.

To participate in the BDD program, servicemembers must:
1. have at least 60 days, but not more than 180 days, remaining on active duty.
2. have a known date of separation or retirement.
3. provide VA with service treatment records, originals or photocopies.
4. be available to complete all necessary examinations prior to leaving the point of separation.

Quick Start is offered to servicemembers who have less than 60 days remaining on active duty or are unable to complete the necessary examinations prior to leaving the point of separation.

To participate in the Quick Start Program, servicemembers must:
1. have at least one day remaining on active duty.
2. have a known date of separation or retirement.
3. provide VA with service treatment records, originals or photocopies.

Servicemembers should contact the local Transition Assistance Office or Army Career Alumni Program Center to schedule appointments to attend VA benefits briefings and learn how to initiate a pre-discharge claim. Servicemembers can obtain more information by calling VA toll-free at 1-800-827-1000 or by visiting www.vba.va.gov/predischarge.

Federal Recovery Coordination Program

The Federal Recovery Coordination Program, a joint program of DOD and VA, helps coordinate and access federal, state and local programs, benefits and services for seriously wounded, ill, and injured Service Members, and their families through recovery, rehabilitation, and reintegration into the community.

Federal Recovery Coordinators (FRCs) have the delegated authority for oversight and coordination of the clinical and non-clinical care identified in each client's Federal Individual Recovery Plan (FIRP). Working with a variety of case managers, FRCs assist their clients in reaching their FIRP goals. FRCs remain with their clients as long as they are needed regardless of the client's location, duty or health status. In doing so, they often serve as the central point of contact and provide transition support for their clients.

Military Services Provide Pre-Separation Counseling

Servicemembers may receive pre-separation counseling 24 months prior to retirement or 12 months prior to separation from active duty. These sessions present information on education, training, employment assistance, National Guard and reserve programs, medical benefits, and financial assistance.

Verification of Military Experience and Training

The Verification of Military Experience and Training (VMET) Document, DD Form 2586, helps servicemembers verify previous experience and training to potential employers, negotiate credits at schools, and obtain certificates or licenses. VMET documents are available only through Army, Navy, Air Force and Marine Corps Transition Support Offices and are intended for servicemembers who have at least six months of active service. Servicemembers should obtain VMET documents from their Transition Support Office within 12 months of separation or 24 months of retirement.

Transition Bulletin Board

To find business opportunities, a calendar of transition seminars, job fairs, information on veterans associations, transition services, training and education opportunities, as well as other announcements, visit the Web site at www.turbotab.org

DOD Transportal

To find locations and phone numbers of all Transition Assistance Offices as well as mini-courses on conducting successful job-search campaigns, writing resumes, using the Internet to find a job, and links to job search and recruiting Web sites, visit the DOD Transportal at www.veteranprograms.com/index.html

Educational and Vocational Counseling

The Vocational Rehabilitation and Employment (VR&E) Program provides educational and vocational counseling to servicemembers, veterans, and certain dependents (U.S.C. Title 38, Section 3697) at no charge. These counseling services are designed to help an individual choose a vocational direction, determine the course needed to achieve the chosen goal, and evaluate the career possibilities open to them.

Assistance may include interest and aptitude testing, occupational exploration, setting occupational goals, locating the right type of training program, and exploring educational or training facilities which can be utilized to achieve an occupational goal.

Counseling services include, but are not limited to, educational and vocational counseling and guidance; testing; analysis of and recommendations to improve job-marketing skills; identification of employment, training, and financial aid resources; and referrals to other agencies providing these services.

Eligibility: Educational and vocational counseling services are available during the period the individual is on active duty with the armed forces and is within 180 days of the estimated date of his or her discharge or release from active duty. The projected discharge must be under conditions other than dishonorable.

Servicemembers are eligible even if they are only considering whether or not they will continue as members of the armed forces. Veterans are eligible if not more than one year has elapsed since the date they were last discharged or released from active duty. Individuals who are eligible for VA education benefits may receive educational and vocational counseling at any time during their eligibility period. This service is based on having eligibility for a VA program such as Chapter 30 (Montgomery GI Bill); Chapter 31 (Vocational Rehabilitation and Employment); Chapter 32 (Veterans Education Assistance Program – VEAP); Chapter 33 (Post-9/11 GI Bill); Chapter 35 (Dependents' Education Assistance Program) for certain spouses and dependent children; Chapter 18 (Spina Bifida Program) for certain dependent children; and Chapter 1606 and 1607 of Title 10.

Veterans and servicemembers may apply for counseling services using VA Form 28-8832, Application for Counseling. Veterans and servicemembers may also write a letter expressing a desire for counseling services.

Upon receipt of either type of request for counseling from an eligible individual, an appointment for counseling will be scheduled. Counseling services are provided to eligible persons at no charge.

Veterans' Workforce Investment Program
Recently separated veterans and those with service-connected disabilities, significant barriers to employment or who served on active duty during a period in which a campaign or expedition badge was authorized can contact the nearest state employment office for employment help through the Veterans Workforce Investment Program. The program may be conducted through state or local public agencies, community organizations or private, nonprofit organizations.

State Employment Services
Veterans can find employment information, education and training opportunities, job counseling, job search workshops, and resume preparation assistance at state Workforce Career or One-Stop Centers. These offices also have specialists to help disabled veterans find employment.

Unemployment Compensation
Veterans who do not begin civilian employment immediately after leaving military service may receive weekly unemployment compensation for a limited time. The amount and duration of payments are determined by individual states. Apply by contacting the nearest state employment office listed in your local telephone directory.

Veterans Preference for Federal Jobs

Since the time of the Civil War, veterans of the U.S. armed forces have been given some degree of preference in appointments to federal jobs. Veterans' preference in its present form comes from the Veterans' Preference Act of 1944, as amended, and now codified in Title 5, United States Code. By law, veterans who are disabled or who served on active duty in the U.S. armed forces during certain specified time periods or in military campaigns are entitled to preference over others when hiring from competitive lists of eligible candidates, and also in retention during a reduction in force (RIF).

To receive preference, a veteran must have been discharged or released from active duty in the U.S. armed forces under honorable conditions (honorable or general discharge). Preference is also provided for certain widows and widowers of deceased veterans who died in service; spouses of service-connected disabled veterans; and mothers of veterans who died under honorable conditions on active duty or have permanent and total service-connected disabilities. For each of these preferences, there are specific criteria that must be met in order to be eligible to receive the veterans' preference.

Recent changes in Title 5 clarify veterans' preference eligibility criteria for National Guard and Reserve members. Veterans eligible for preference include National Guard and Reserve members who served on active duty as defined by Title 38 at any time in the armed forces for a period of more than 180 consecutive days, any part of which occurred during the period beginning on Sept.11, 2001, and ending on the date prescribed by Presidential proclamation or by law as the last date of OEF/OIF. The National Guard and Reserve service members must have been discharged or released from active duty in the armed forces under honorable conditions.

Another recent change involves veterans who earned the Global War on Terrorism Expeditionary Medal for service in OEF/OIF. Under Title 5, service on active duty in the armed forces during a war or in a campaign or expedition for which a campaign badge has been authorized also qualifies for veterans' preference. Any Armed Forces Expeditionary medal or campaign badge qualifies for preference. Medal holders must have served continuously for 24 months or the full period called or ordered to active duty.

As of December 2005, veterans who received the Global War on

Terrorism Expeditionary Medal are entitled to veterans' preference if otherwise eligible. For additional information, visit the Office of Personnel Management (OPM) Web site at www.opm.gov/veterans/html/vetguide.asp#2.

Veterans' preference does not require an agency to use any particular appointment process. Agencies can pick candidates from a number of different special hiring authorities or through a variety of different sources. For example, the agency can reinstate a former federal employee, transfer someone from another agency, reassign someone from within the agency, make a selection under merit promotion procedures or through open, competitive exams, or appoint someone noncompetitively under special authority such as a Veterans Readjustment Appointment or special authority for 30 percent or more disabled veterans. The decision on which hiring authority the agency desires to use rests solely with the agency.

When applying for federal jobs, eligible veterans should claim preference on their application or resume. Veterans should apply for a federal job by contacting the personnel office at the agency in which they wish to work. For more information, visit www.usajobs.opm.gov/ for job openings or help creating a federal resume.

Veterans' Employment Opportunities Act: When an agency accepts applications from outside its own workforce, the Veterans' Employment Opportunities Act of 1998 allows preference eligible candidates or veterans to compete for these vacancies under merit promotion procedures.

Veterans who are selected are given career or career-conditional appointments. Veterans are those who have been separated under honorable conditions from the U.S. armed forces with three or more years of continuous active service. For information, visit www.usajobs.opm.gov or www.fedshirevets.gov.

Veterans' Recruitment Appointment: Allows federal agencies to appoint eligible veterans to jobs without competition. These appointments can be converted to career or career-conditional positions after two years of satisfactory work. Veterans should apply directly to the agency where they wish to work. For information,www.fedshirevets.gov/.

Small Businesses

VA's Center for Veterans Enterprise helps veterans interested in forming or expanding small businesses and helps VA contracting offices identify veteran-owned small businesses. For information, write the U.S. Department of Veterans Affairs (OOVE), 810 Vermont Avenue, N.W., Washington, DC 20420-0001, call toll-free 1-866-584-2344 or visit www.vetbiz.gov/.

Small Business Contracts: Like other federal agencies, VA is required to place a portion of its contracts and purchases with small and disadvantaged businesses. VA has a special office to help small and disadvantaged businesses get information on VA acquisition opportunities. For information, write the U.S. Department of Veterans Affairs (OOSB), 810 Vermont Avenue, N.W., Washington, DC 20420-0001, call toll-free 1-800-949-8387 or visit www.va.gov/osdbu/.

Chapter 11

Dependents and Survivors Health Care

Health Care Benefits

Under the Civilian Health and Medical Program of the Department of Veterans Affairs (CHAMPVA), certain dependents and survivors can receive reimbursement for most medical expenses – inpatient, outpatient, mental health, prescription medication, skilled nursing care and durable medical equipment.

Eligibility: To be eligible for CHAMPVA, an individual cannot be eligible for TRICARE (the medical program for civilian dependents provided by DoD) and must be one of the following:
1. The spouse or child of a Veteran whom VA has rated permanently and totally disabled due to a service-connected disability.
2. The surviving spouse or child of a Veteran who died from a VA-rated service-connected disability, or who, at the time of death, was rated permanently and totally disabled.
3. The surviving spouse or child of a Veteran who died on active duty service and in the line of duty, not due to misconduct. However, in most of these cases, these family members are eligible for TRICARE, not CHAMPVA.

A surviving spouse under age 55 who remarries loses CHAMPVA eligibility on midnight of the date of remarriage. He/she may re-establish eligibility if the remarriage ends by death, divorce or annulment effective the first day of the month following the termination of the remarriage or Dec. 1, 1999, whichever is later. A surviving spouse who remarries after age 55 does not lose eligibility upon remarriage.

For those who have Medicare entitlement, CHAMPVA is secondary payer to Medicare. For additional information, contact the VA Health Administration Center, CHAMPVA, P.O. Box 469028, Denver, CO 80246, call 1-800-733-8387 or visit the Web site at www.va.gov/hac/forbeneficiaries/champva/champva.asp.

Many VA health care facilities provide services to CHAMPVA beneficiaries under the CHAMPVA In-house Treatment Initiative (CITI) program. Contact the nearest VA health care facility to determine if it participates. Those who use a CITI facility incur no cost for services; however, services are provided on a space-available basis, after the needs of Veterans are met. Not all services are available at all times. The coverage of services is dependent upon the CHAMPVA benefit coverage. CHAMPVA beneficiaries who are covered by Medicare cannot use CITI.

Children Born with Spina Bifida to Certain Vietnam or Korean Veterans: The Spina Bifida Program (SB) is a health benefit program administered by the Department of Veterans Affairs for women. Vietnam and certain Korean Veterans' birth children who have been diagnosed with spina bifida (except spina bifida occulta). The SB program provides reimbursement for medical services and supplies. Effective October 10, 2008, there was a change to Public Law 110-387, Section 408. As a result of this change, medical services and supplies for spina bifida beneficiaries are no longer limited to the spina bifida condition. The VA's Health Administration Center in Denver, Colorado, manages the SB Program, including the authorization of benefits and the subsequent processing and payment of claims. For more information about spina bifida health care benefits, call 1-888-820-1756 or visit the Web site at www.va.gov/hac/forbeneficiaries/spina/spina.asp

Eligibility: To be eligible for the SB Program, you must be eligible for a monetary award under the Veterans Benefit Administration (VBA). The Denver VA Regional Office makes determination regarding this entitlement. The VBA notifies the VA Health Administration Center after an award is made and the eligible child is enrolled in SB.

Children of Women Vietnam Veterans (CWVV) Born with Certain Birth Defects: The CWVV Health Care Program is a federal health benefits program administered by the Department of Veterans Affairs for children of women Vietnam Veterans born with certain birth defects. The CWVV Program provides reimbursement for medical care related to certain conditions associated with birth defects except for spina bifida based on a fee for service. For more information about benefits for children with birth defects, call 1-888-820-1756 or visit the Web site at www.va.gov/hac/forbeneficiaries and select Spina Bifida/Children of Women Vietnam Veterans (CWVV.)

Eligibility: To be eligible for the CWVV Program, you must have received an award under VBA. The Denver VA Regional Office makes determination regarding this entitlement. The VBA notifies the VA Health Administration Center after an award is made and the eligible child is enrolled in CWVV.

Bereavement Counseling

VA Vet Centers provide bereavement counseling to all family members including spouses, children, parents, and siblings of servicemembers who die while on active duty. This includes federally activated members of the National Guard and reserve components. Bereavement services may be accessed by calling (202) 461-6530.

Bereavement Counseling related to Veterans: Bereavement counseling is available through any Veterans Health Administration medical center to immediate family members of veterans who die unexpectedly or while participating in a VA hospice or similar program, as long as the immediate family members had been receiving family support services in connection with or in furtherance of the veteran's treatment. (In other cases, bereavement counseling is available to the veteran's legal guardian or the individual with whom the veteran had certified an intention to live, as long as the guardian or individual had been receiving covered family support services.) This bereavement counseling is of limited duration and may only be authorized up to 60 days. However, VA medical center directors have authority to approve a longer period of time when medically indicated. Contact the Social Work Service at your closest VA Medical Center to access bereavement counseling services.

Chapter 12

Dependents and Survivors Benefits

Death Gratuity Payment

Military services provide payment, called a death gratuity, in the amount of $100,000 to the next of kin of servicemembers who die while on active duty (including those who die within 120 days of separation) as a result of service-connected injury or illness. If there is no surviving spouse or child, then parents or siblings designated as next of kin by the servicemember may be provided the payment. The payment is made by the last military command of the deceased. If the beneficiary is not paid automatically, application may be made to the military service concerned.

Dependency and Indemnity Compensation

Eligibility: For a survivor to be eligible for Dependency and Indemnity Compensation (DIC), the veteran's death must have resulted from one of the following causes:

1. A disease or injury incurred or aggravated in the line of duty while on active duty or active duty for training.
2. An injury, heart attack, cardiac arrest, or stroke incurred or aggravated in the line of duty while on inactive duty for training.
3. A service-connected disability or a condition directly related to a service-connected disability.

DIC also may be paid to certain survivors of veterans who were totally disabled from service-connected conditions at the time of death, even though their service-connected disabilities did not cause their deaths. The survivor qualifies if the veteran was:

1. Continuously rated totally disabled for a period of 10 years immediately preceding death; or
2. Continuously rated totally disabled from the date of military discharge and for at least 5 years immediately preceding death; or
3. A former POW who died after Sept. 30, 1999, and who was continuously rated totally disabled for a period of at least one year immediately preceding death.

Payments will be offset by any amount received from judicial proceedings brought on by the veteran's death. The veteran's discharge must have been under conditions other than dishonorable.

Payments for Deaths After Jan. 1, 1993: Surviving spouses of veterans who died on or after Jan. 1, 1993, receive a basic rate, plus additional payments for dependent children, for the aid and attendance of another person if they are patients in a nursing home or require the regular assistance of another person, or if they are permanently housebound.

DIC Payment Rates for Surviving Spouses*

Allowances	Monthly Rate
Basic Payment Rate	$1,154
Additional Allowances:	
Each Dependent Child	$286
Aid and Attendance	$286
Housebound	$135

Veterans who died on or after Jan. 1, 1993.

Special Allowances: Add $233 if the veteran was totally disabled eight continuous years prior to death.

Add $250 to the additional allowance if there are dependent children under age 18 for the initial two years of entitlement for DIC awards commencing on or after Jan. 1, 2005.

Payments for Deaths Prior to Jan. 1, 1993: Surviving spouses of veterans who died prior to Jan. 1, 1993, receive an amount based on the deceased's military pay grade.

Death Pension Rates

Recipient of Pension	Maximum Annual Rate
Surviving spouse	$7,933
(With dependent child)	$10,385
Permanently housebound	$9,696
(With dependent child)	$12,144
Needs regular aid & attendance	$12,681

(With dependent child)	$15,587
Each additional dependent child	$2,020
Pension for each surviving child	$2,020

Parents' DIC: VA provides an income-based monthly benefit to the surviving parent(s) of a servicemember or veteran whose death was service-related. When countable income exceeds the limit set by law, no benefits are payable. The spouse's income must also be included if living with a spouse.

A spouse may be the other parent of the deceased veteran, or a spouse from remarriage. Unreimbursed medical expenses may be used to reduce countable income. Benefit rates and income limits change annually.

DIC Rates for Surviving Spouses*

Enlisted	Rate	Warrant Officer	Rate	Officer	Rate
E-1	$1,154	W-1	$1,219	O-1	$1,219
E-2	$1,154	W-2	$1,267	O-2	$1,260
E-3	$1,154	W-3	$1,305	O-3	$1,347
E-4	$1,154	W-4	$1,380	O-4	$1,427
E-5	$1,154			O-5	$1,571
E-6	$1,154			O-6	$1,771
E-7	$1,194			O-7	$1,912
E-8	$1,260			O-8	$2,100
E-9	$1,314			O-9	$2,246
				O-10	$2,463

*Veterans who died prior to Jan. 1, 1993.

Restored Entitlement Program for Survivors: Survivors of veterans who died of service-connected causes incurred or aggravated prior to Aug. 13, 1981, may be eligible for a special benefit payable in addition to any other benefits to which the family may be entitled. The amount of the benefit is based on information provided by the Social Security Administration.

Death Pension

VA provides pensions to low-income surviving spouses and unmarried children of deceased veterans with wartime service.

Eligibility: To be eligible, spouses must not have remarried and children must be under age 18, or under age 23 if attending a VA-approved school, or have become permanently incapable of self-support because of disability before age 18.

The veteran must have been discharged under conditions other than dishonorable and must have had 90 days or more of active military service, at least one day of which was during a period of war, or a service-connected disability justifying discharge. Longer periods of service may be required for veterans who entered active duty on or after Sept. 8, 1980, or Oct. 16, 1981, if an officer. If the veteran died in service but not in the line of duty, the death pension may be payable if the veteran completed at least two years of honorable service.

Children who become incapable of self-support because of a disability before age 18 may be eligible for the death pension as long as the condition exists, unless the child marries or the child's income exceeds the applicable limit.

A surviving spouse may be entitled to a higher income limit if living in a nursing home, in need of the aid and attendance of another person, or permanently housebound.

Payment: The death pension provides a monthly payment to bring an eligible person's income to a level established by law. The payment is reduced by the annual income from other sources such as Social Security. The payment may be increased if the recipient has unreimbursed medical expenses that can be deducted from countable income.

Dependents' Educational Assistance

Eligibility: VA provides educational assistance to qualifying dependents as follows:
1. The spouse or child of a servicemember or veteran who either died of a service-connected disability, or who has permanent and total service-connected disability, or who died while such a disability existed.
2. The spouse or child of a servicemember listed for more than

90 days as currently Missing in Action (MIA), captured in the line of duty by a hostile force, or detained or interned by a foreign government or power.

3. The spouse or child of a servicemember who is hospitalized or is receiving outpatient care or treatment for a disability that is determined to be totally and permanently disabling, incurred or aggravated due to active duty, and for which the service member is likely to be discharged from military service.

Surviving spouses lose eligibility if they remarry before age 57 or are living with another person who has been held out publicly as their spouse. They can regain eligibility if their remarriage ends by death or divorce or if they cease living with the person. Dependent children do not lose eligibility if the surviving spouse remarries. Visit www.gibill.va.gov/ for more information.

Period of Eligibility: The period of eligibility for veterans' spouses expires 10 years from either the date they become eligible or the date of the veteran's death. VA may grant an extension. Children generally must be between the ages of 18 and 26 to receive educational benefits, though extensions may be granted.

The period of eligibility for spouses of servicemembers who died on active duty expires 20 years from the date of death. This is a change in law that became effective Dec. 10, 2004. Spouses of servicemembers who died on active duty whose 10-year eligibility period expired before Dec. 10, 2004, now have 20 years from the date of death to use educational benefits. Effective Oct. 10, 2008, Public Law 110-389 provides a 20-year period of eligibility for spouses of veterans with a permanent and total service-connected disability rating effective within 3 years of release from active duty.

Payments: The payment rate effective Oct. 1, 2009, is $925 a month for full-time school attendance, with lesser amounts for part-time. Benefits are paid for full-time training up to 45 months or the equivalent in part-time training.

Training Available: Benefits may be awarded for pursuit of associate, bachelor, or graduate degrees at colleges and universities; independent study; cooperative training study abroad certificate or diploma from business, technical or vocational schools, apprenticeships, on-the-job training programs; and farm cooperative courses.

Benefits for correspondence courses under certain conditions are available to spouses only.

Beneficiaries without high-school degrees can pursue secondary schooling, and those with a deficiency in a subject may receive tutorial assistance if enrolled half-time or more.

Marine Gunnery Sergeant John David Fry Scholarship

Children of those who die in the line of duty on or since September 11, 2001, are potentially eligible to use Post-9/11 GI Bill benefits. Refer to Chapter 4, "Education and Training", for more details.

Work-Study: Participants who train at the three-quarter or full-time rate may be eligible for a work-study program in which they work for VA and receive hourly wages. The types of work allowed include:
1. Outreach services.
2. VA paperwork.
3. Work at national or state veterans' cemeteries.
4. Work at VA medical centers or state veterans' homes.
5. Other VA-approved activities.

Counseling: VA may provide counseling to help participants pursue an educational or vocational objective.

Special Benefits: Dependents over age 14 with physical or mental disabilities that impair their ability to pursue an education may receive specialized vocational or restorative training, including speech and voice correction, language retraining, lip reading, auditory training, Braille reading and writing, and similar programs. Certain disabled or surviving spouses are also eligible.

Montgomery GI Bill (MGIB) Death Benefit: VA will pay a special MGIB death benefit to a designated survivor in the event of the service-connected death of a servicemember while on active duty or within one year after discharge or release. The deceased must either have been entitled to educational assistance under the MGIB program or a participant in the program who would have been so entitled but for the high school diploma or length-of-service requirement. The amount paid will be equal to the participant's actual military pay reduction, less any education benefits paid.

Children of Vietnam Veterans Born with Certain Birth DefectsChildren

Children of Vietnam Veterans Born with Certain Birth Defects or Children of Vietnam or Korean Veterans Born with Spina Bifida: Biological children of male and female Veterans who served in Vietnam at any time during the period beginning January 9, 1962 and ending May 7, 1975, or who served in or near the Korean demilitarized zone (DMZ) during the period beginning September 1, 1967 and ending August 31, 1971, Children of Vietnam Veterans born with certain birth defects may be eligible for a monthly monetary allowance, and vocational training if reasonably feasible.

The law defines "child" as the natural child of a Vietnam Veteran, regardless of age or marital status. The child must have been conceived after the date on which the Veteran first entered the Republic of Vietnam. For more information about benefits for children with birth defects, visit www.va.gov/hac/forbeneficiaries/spina/spina.asp.

A monetary allowance is paid at one of three disability levels based on the neurological manifestations that define the severity of disability: impairment of the functioning of extremities, impairment of bowel or bladder function, and impairment of intellectual functioning.

	Level I	Level II	Level III
Monthly Rate*	$286	$984	$1,687

*Effective Dec. 1, 2008

Children of Women Vietnam Veterans Born with Certain Birth Defects: Biological children of women Veterans who served in Vietnam at any time during the period beginning on February 28, 1961 and ending on May 7, 1975, may be eligible for certain benefits because of birth defects associated with the mother's service in Vietnam that resulted in a permanent physical or mental disability.

The covered birth defects do not include conditions due to family disorders, birth-related injuries, or fetal or neonatal infirmities with well-established causes. A monetary allowance is paid at one of four disability levels based on the child's degree of permanent disability.

VA Benefits for Children of Women Vietnam Veterans Born with Certain Birth Defects

	Level I	Level II	Level III	Level V
Monthly Rate*	$131	$286	$984	$1,678

Effective Dec. 1, 2008

Vocational Training: VA provides vocational training, rehabilitation services, and employment assistance to help these children prepare for and attain suitable employment. To qualify, an applicant must be a child receiving a VA monthly allowance for spina bifida or another covered birth defect and for whom VA has determined that achievement of a vocational goal is reasonably feasible. A child may not begin vocational training before his/her 18th birthday or the date he/she completes secondary schooling, whichever comes first. Depending on need and eligibility, a child may be provided up to 24 months of full-time training with the possibility of an extension of up to 24 months if it is needed to achieve the identified employment goal.

VA Home Loan Guaranty
A VA loan guaranty to acquire a home may be available to an unmarried spouse of a veteran or servicemember who died as a result of service-connected disabilities, a surviving spouse who remarries after age 57, or to a spouse of a servicemember officially listed as MIA or who is currently a POW for more than 90 days. Spouses of those listed MIA/POW are limited to one loan.

"No-Fee" Passports
"No-fee" passports are available to immediate family members (spouse, children, parents, brothers and sisters) for the expressed purpose of visiting their loved one's grave or memorialization site at an American military cemetery on foreign soil. For additional information, write to the American Battle Monuments Commission, Courthouse Plaza II, Suite 500, 2300 Clarendon Blvd., Arlington, VA 22201, or telephone 703-696-6897, or visit the Web site at www.abmc.gov/home.php.

Chapter 13
Appeals of VA Claims Decisions

Veterans and other claimants for VA benefits have the right to appeal decisions made by a VA regional office, medical center or National Cemetery Administration (NCA) office. Typical issues appealed are disability compensation, pension, education benefits, recovery of overpayments, reimbursement for unauthorized medical services, and denial of burial and memorial benefits.

A claimant has one year from the date of the notification of a VA decision to file an appeal. The first step in the appeal process is for a claimant to file a written notice of disagreement with the VA regional office, medical center or NCA office that made the decision.

Following receipt of the written notice, VA will furnish the claimant a "Statement of the Case" describing what facts, laws, and regulations were used in deciding the case. To complete the request for appeal, the claimant must file a "Substantive Appeal" within 60 days of the mailing of the Statement of the Case, or within one year from the date VA mailed its decision, whichever period ends later.

Board of Veterans' Appeals

The Board of Veterans' Appeals makes decisions on appeals on behalf of the Secretary of Veterans Affairs. Although it is not required, a veterans service organization, an agent, or an attorney may represent a claimant. Appellants may present their cases in person to a member of the Board at a hearing in Washington, D.C., at a VA regional office or by videoconference.

Decisions made by the Board can be found on the Web site at www.va.gov/vbs/bva/. The pamphlet, "Understanding the Appeal Process," is available on the Web site or may be requested by writing: Hearings and Transcription Unit (014HRG), Board of Veterans' Appeals, 811 Vermont Avenue, NW, Washington, DC 20420.

U.S. Court of Appeals for Veterans Claims

A final Board of Veterans' Appeals decision that does not grant a claimant the benefits desired may be appealed to the U.S. Court of Appeals for Veterans Claims, an independent court, not part of the Department of Veterans Affairs.

Notice of an appeal must be received by the court with a postmark that is within 120 days after the Board of Veterans' Appeals mailed its decision. The court reviews the record considered by the Board of Veterans' Appeals. It does not hold trials or receive new evidence.

Appellants may represent themselves before the court or have lawyers or approved agents as representatives. Oral argument is held only at the direction of the court. Either party may appeal a decision of the court to the U.S. Court of Appeals for the Federal Circuit and may seek review in the Supreme Court of the United States.

Published decisions, case status information, rules and procedures, and other special announcements can be found on the court's Web site at www.vetapp.gov/. The court's decisions can also be found in West's Veterans Appeals Reporter, and on the Westlaw and LEXIS online services. For questions, write the Clerk of the Court, 625 Indiana Ave. NW, Suite 900, Washington, DC 20004, or call (202) 501-5970.

Chapter 14
Military Medals and Records

Replacing Military Medals

Medals awarded while in active service are issued by the individual military services if requested by veterans or their next of kin. Requests for replacement medals, decorations, and awards should be directed to the branch of the military in which the veteran served. However, for Air Force (including Army Air Corps) and Army veterans, the National Personnel Records Center (NPRC) verifies awards and forwards requests and verification to appropriate services.

Requests for replacement medals should be submitted on Standard Form 180, "Request Pertaining To Military Records," which may be obtained at VA offices or the Internet at www.va.gov/vaforms/. Forms, addresses, and other information on requesting medals can be found on the Military Personnel Records section of NPRC's Web site at www.archives.gov/st-louis/military-personnel/index.html. For questions, call Military Personnel Records at (314) 801-0800 or e-mail questions to: MPR.center@nara.gov.

When requesting medals, type or clearly print the veteran's full name, include the veteran's branch of service, service number or Social Security number and provide the veteran's exact or approximate dates of military service. The request must contain the signature of the veteran or next of kin if the veteran is deceased. If available, include a copy of the discharge or separation document, WDAGO Form 53-55 or DD Form 214.

Replacing Military Records

If discharge or separation documents are lost, veterans or the next of kin of deceased veterans may obtain duplicate copies by completing forms found on the Internet at www.archives.gov/research/index.html and mailing or faxing them to the NPRC.

Alternatively, write the National Personnel Records Center, Military

Personnel Records, 9700 Page Blvd., St. Louis, MO 63132-5100. Specify that a duplicate separation document is needed. The veteran's full name should be printed or typed so that it can be read clearly, but the request must also contain the signature of the veteran or the signature of the next of kin, if the veteran is deceased. Include the veteran's branch of service, service number or Social Security number and exact or approximate dates and years of service. Use Standard Form 180, "Request Pertaining To Military Records."

It is not necessary to request a duplicate copy of a veteran's discharge or separation papers solely for the purpose of filing a claim for VA benefits. If complete information about the veteran's service is furnished on the application, VA will obtain verification of service.

Correcting of Military Records

The secretary of a military department, acting through a Board for Correction of Military Records, has authority to change any military record when necessary to correct an error or remove an injustice. A correction board may consider applications for correction of a military record, including a review of a discharge issued by court-martial.

The veteran, survivor or legal representative must file a request for correction within three years after discovering an alleged error or injustice. The board may excuse failure to file within this time, however, if it finds it would be in the interest of justice. It is an applicant's responsibility to show why the filing of the application was delayed and why it would be in the interest of justice for the board to consider it despite the delay.

To justify a correction, it is necessary to show to the satisfaction of the board that the alleged entry or omission in the records was in error or unjust. Applications should include all available evidence, such as signed statements of witnesses or a brief of arguments supporting the correction. Application is made with DD Form 149, available at VA offices, veterans organizations or visit www.dtic.mil/whs/directives/infomgt/forms/formsprogram.htm.

Review of Discharge from Military Service

Each of the military services maintains a discharge review board with authority to change, correct or modify discharges or dismissals not issued by a sentence of a general court-martial. The board has no authority to address medical discharges.

The veteran or, if the veteran is deceased or incompetent, the surviving spouse, next of kin or legal representative, may apply for a review of discharge by writing to the military department concerned, using DD Form 293 -- "Application for the Review of Discharge from the Armed Forces of the United States." This form may be obtained at a VA regional office, from veterans organizations or from the Internet at www.dtic.mil/whs/directives/infomgt/forms/formsprogram.htm.

However, if the discharge was more than 15 years ago, a veteran must petition the appropriate Service's Board for Correction of Military Records using DD Form 149 -- "Application for Correction of Military Records Under the Provisions of Title 10, U.S. Code, Section 1552." A discharge review is conducted by a review of an applicant's record and, if requested, by a hearing before the board.

Discharges awarded as a result of a continuous period of unauthorized absence in excess of 180 days make persons ineligible for VA benefits regardless of action taken by discharge review boards, unless VA determines there were compelling circumstances for the absence. Boards for the Correction of Military Records also may consider such cases.

Veterans with disabilities incurred or aggravated during active duty may qualify for medical or related benefits regardless of separation and characterization of service. Veterans separated administratively under other than honorable conditions may request that their discharge be reviewed for possible recharacterization, provided they file their appeal within 15 years of the date of separation.

Questions regarding the review of a discharge should be addressed to the appropriate discharge review board at the address listed on DD Form 293.

Chapter 15

Benefits Provided by Other Federal Agencies

USDA Provides Loans for Farms and Homes

The U.S. Department of Agriculture (USDA) provides loans and guarantees to buy, improve or operate farms. Loans and guarantees are generally available for housing in towns with a population up to 20,000. Applications from veterans have preference. For further information, contact Farm Service Agency or Rural Development, USDA, 1400 Independence Ave., S.W., Washington, DC 20250, or apply at local Department of Agriculture offices, usually located in county seats.

Housing and Urban Development (HUDVET)

Housing and Urban Development (HUD) sponsors the Veteran Resource Center (HUDVET), which works with national veterans service organizations to serve as a general information center on all HUD-sponsored housing and community development programs and services. To contact HUDVET, call 1-800-998-9999, TDD 800-483-2209, or visit its Web site at www.hud.gov/hudvet.

Veterans Receive Naturalization Preference

Honorable active-duty service in the U.S. armed forces during a designated period of hostility allows an individual to naturalize without being required to establish any periods of residence or physical presence in the United States. A servicemember who was in the United States, certain territories, or aboard an American public vessel at the time of enlistment, re-enlistment, extension of enlistment or induction, may naturalize even if he or she is not a lawful permanent resident.

On July 3, 2002, the president issued Executive Order 13269 establishing a new period of hostility for naturalization purposes beginning Sept. 11, 2001, and continuing until a date designated by a future Executive Order. Qualifying members of the armed forces who have served at any time during a specified period of hostility may immediately apply for naturalization using the current application – Form N-400 – "Application for Naturalization." Additional information about filing and requirement fees and designated periods of hostility are available on the U.S. Citizenship and Immigration Services (USCIS) Web site at www.uscis.gov.

Individuals who served honorably in the U.S. armed forces, but were no longer serving on active duty status as of Sept. 11, 2001, may still be naturalized without having to comply with the residence and physical presence requirements for naturalization if they filed Form N-400 while still serving in the U.S. armed forces or within six months of termination of their active duty service.

An individual who files the application for naturalization after the six-month period following termination of active-duty service is not exempt from the residence and physical presence requirements, but can count any period of active-duty service towards the residence and physical presence requirements. Individuals seeking naturalization under this provision must establish that they are lawful permanent residents (such status not having been lost, rescinded or abandoned) and that they served honorably in the U.S. armed forces for at least one year.

If a servicemember dies as a result of injury or disease incurred or aggravated by service during a time of combat, the servicemember's survivor(s) can apply for the deceased servicemember to receive posthumous citizenship at any time within two years of the servicemember's death. The issuance of a posthumous certificate of citizenship does not confer U.S. citizenship on surviving relatives. However, a non-U.S. citizen spouse or qualifying family member may file for certain immigration benefits and services based upon their relationship to a servicemember who died during hostilities or a non-citizen servicemember who died during hostilities and was later granted posthumous citizenship.

For additional information, USCIS has developed a web page – www. uscis.gov/military – that contains information and links to services specifically for the military and their families. Members of the U.S. military and their families stationed around the world can also call USCIS for help with immigration services and benefits using a dedicated, toll-free Military help line at 1-877-CIS-4MIL (1-877-247-4645).

Small Business Administration (SBA)

Historically, veterans do very well as small business entrepreneurs. Veterans interested in entrepreneurship and small business ownership should look to the U.S. Small Business Administration's Office of Veterans Business Development (www.sba.gov/vets) for assistance. OVBD conducts comprehensive outreach to veterans, service-disabled veterans and Reserve Component members of the U.S. military. OVBD also provides assistance to veteran- and reservist-owned small businesses. SBA is the primary federal agency responsible for assisting veterans who own or are considering starting their own small businesses.

Among the services provided by SBA are business-planning assistance, counseling and training through community based Veterans Business Outreach Centers. For more information, go to www.sba.gov/aboutsba/sbaprograms/ovbd/OVBD_VBOP.html. More than 1,000 university-based Small Business Development Centers; nearly 400 SCORE chapters (www.score.org/veteran.html) with 11,000 volunteer counselors, many of whom are veterans; and 100 Women's Business Centers.

SBA also manages a range of special small business lending programs at thousands of locations, ranging from Micro Loans to the Military-community-targeted Patriot Express Pilot Loan, to venture capital and Surety Bond Guarantees (www.sba.gov/services/financialassistance/index.html). Veterans also participate in all SBA federal procurement programs, including a special 3 percent federal procurement goal specifically for service-connected disabled veterans, and SBA supports veterans and others participating in international trade.

A special Military Reservist Economic Injury Disaster Loan (www.sba.gov/reservists) is available for self-employed Reservists whose small businesses may be damaged through the absence of the owner or an essential employee as a result of Title 10 activation to Active Duty.

A Veterans Business Development Officer is stationed at every SBA District Office to act as a guide to veterans, and SBA offers a full range of self-paced small business planning assistance at www.sba.gov/survey/checklist/index.cgi for veterans, reservists, discharging service members and their families. Information about the full range of services can be found at www.sba.gov/vets/ and at www.sba.gov/

reservists/, or by calling 202-205-6773 or 1-800-U-ASK-SBA (1-800-827-5722).

Social Security Administration

Monthly retirement, disability and survivor benefits under Social Security are payable to veterans and dependents if the veteran has earned enough work credits under the program. Upon the veteran's death, a one-time payment of $255 also may be made to the veteran's spouse or child. In addition, a veteran may qualify at age 65 for Medicare's hospital insurance and medical insurance. Medicare protection is available to people who have received Social Security disability benefits for 24 months, and to insured people and their dependents who need dialysis or kidney transplants, or who have amyotrophic lateral sclerosis (more commonly known as Lou Gehrig's disease).

Since 1957, military service earnings for active duty (including active duty for training) have counted toward Social Security and those earnings are already on Social Security records. Since 1988, inactive duty service in the Reserve Component (such as weekend drills) has also been covered by Social Security. Servicemembers and veterans are credited with $300 credit in additional earnings for each calendar quarter in which they received active duty basic pay after 1956 and before 1978.

Veterans who served in the military from 1978 through 2001 are credited with an additional $100 in earnings for each $300 in active duty basic pay, up to a maximum of $1,200 a year. No additional Social Security taxes are withheld from pay for these extra credits. Veterans who enlisted after Sept. 7, 1980, and did not complete at least 24 months of active duty or their full tour of duty, may not be able to receive the additional earnings. Check with Social Security for details. Additional earnings will no longer be credited for military service periods after 2001.

Also, non-contributory Social Security earnings of $160 a month may be credited to veterans who served after Sept. 15, 1940, and before 1957, including attendance at service academies. For information, call 1-800-772-1213 or visit www.socialsecurity.gov/. (Note: Social Security cannot add these extra earnings to the record until an application is filed for Social Security benefits).

Eligibility for Supplemental Security Income (SSI)

Those 65 or older and those who are blind or otherwise disabled may be eligible for monthly Supplemental Security Income (SSI) payments if they have little or no income or resources. States may supplement the federal payments to eligible persons and may disregard additional income.

Although VA compensation and pension benefits are counted in determining income for SSI purposes, some other income is not counted. Also, not all resources count in determining eligibility. For example, a person's home and the land it is on do not count. Personal effects, household goods, automobiles and life insurance may not count, depending upon their value. Information and help is available at any Social Security office or by calling 1-800-772-1213.

Armed Forces Retirement Homes

Veterans are eligible to live in the Armed Forces Retirement Homes located in Gulfport, Miss., or Washington, D.C., if their active duty military service is at least 50 percent enlisted, warrant officer or limited duty officer if they qualify under one of the following categories:

1. Are 60 years of age or older; and were discharged or released under honorable conditions after 20 or more years of active service.
2. Are determined to be incapable of earning a livelihood because of a service-connected disability incurred in the line of duty.
3. Served in a war theater during a time of war declared by Congress or were eligible for hostile-fire special pay and were discharged or released under honorable conditions; and are determined to be incapable of earning a livelihood because of injuries, disease or disability.
4. Served in a women's component of the armed forces before June 12, 1948; and are determined to be eligible for admission due to compelling personal circumstances.

Eligibility determinations are based on rules prescribed by the Home's Chief Operating Officer. Veterans are not eligible if they have been convicted of a felony or are not free from alcohol, drug or psychiatric problems. Married couples are welcome, but both must be eligible in their own right. At the time of admission, applicants must be capable of living independently.

The Armed Forces Retirement Home is an independent federal agency. For information, call 1-800-332-3527 or 1-800-422-9988, or visit www.afrh.gov/.

*The Gulfport, Miss., facility is scheduled to open in the fall of 2010.

Commissary and Exchange Privileges

Unlimited exchange and commissary store privileges in the United States are available to honorably discharged veterans with a service-connected disability rated at 100 percent, un-remarried surviving spouses of veterans with a service-connected disability rated at 100 percent at the time of death, un-remarried surviving spouses of members or retired members of the armed forces, recipients of the Medal of Honor, and their dependents and orphans. Certification of total disability is done by VA. Reservists and their dependents also may be eligible. Privileges overseas are governed by international law and are available only if agreed upon by the foreign government concerned.

Though these benefits are provided by DOD, VA does provide assistance in completing DD Form 1172, "Application for Uniformed Services Identification and Privilege Card." For detailed information, contact the nearest military installation.

VA Facilities

Patients should call the telephone numbers listed to obtain clinic hours of operation and services.

For more information or to search for a facility near you by zip code, visit www1.va.gov/directory/guide/home.asp?isFlash=1

Under the National Cemeteries listings, the acronym NC is used after the name of the town to designate locations of national cemeteries.

Please send address and telephone number corrections to:

Federal Benefits for Veterans and Dependents (80D)
810 Vermont Ave. NW
Washington, DC 20420

ALABAMA

Regional Office:
Montgomery 36109 (345 Perry Hill Rd., statewide 1-800-827-1000)

VA Medical Centers:
Birmingham 35233 (700 S. 19th St., 205-933-8101 or 800-872-0328)
Montgomery 36109-3798 (215 Perry Hill Rd., 334-272-4670 or 800-214-8387)
Tuscaloosa 35404 (3701 Loop Rd., East, 205-554-2000 or 888-269-3045)
Tuskegee 36083-5001 (2400 Hospital Rd., 334-727-0550 or 800-214-8387)

Clinics:
Bessemer 32055 (975 9th Ave., SW-Suite 400 at UAB West Medical Center West Bessemer, 205-428-3495)
Dothan 36301 (2020 Alexander Dr., 334-673-4166)
Dothan Mental Health Center 36303 (3753 Ross Clark Cir Ste 4, 334-678-1933)
Ft. Rucker 36362 (301 Andrews Ave., 334-727-0550)
Gadsden 35906 (206 Rescia Ave., 256-413-7154)
Huntsville 35801 (301 Governor's Dr., 256-535-3100)
Jasper 35501 (3400 Highway 78 East - Suite #215, 205-221-7384)
Madison 35758 (8075 Madison Blvd., Suite 101, 256-772-6220)
Mobile 36604 (1504 Springhill Ave, 251-219-3900/888-201-0110)
Oxford 36203 (96 Ali Way Creekside South, 256-832-4141)
Sheffield 35660 (Florence Shoals Area Clinic: 422 DD Cox Blvd., 256-381-9055)

Vet Centers:
Birmingham 35233 (1500 5th Ave. S., 205-731-0550)
Mobile 36606 (2577 Government Blvd., 251-478-5906)

National Cemeteries:
Alabama 35115 (3133 Hwy. 119, Montevallo, AL, 205-665-9039)
Fort Mitchell 36856 (553 Hwy. 165, Fort Mitchell, 334-855-4731)
Mobile 36604 (1202 Virginia St., 850-453-4846)

ALASKA

VA Medical Center:
Anchorage 99504 (1201 N. Muldoon Rd., 888-353-7574/907-257-4700)

Clinics:
Fort Wainwright 99703 (Bldg 4076, Neeley Rd., Room 1J-101, Mailing Address: P.O. Box 74570, Fairbanks, AK 99707, 907-361-6370 or 888-353-5242)
Kenai 99669 (11312 Kenai Spur Highway, #39, 907-395-4100 or 1-877-797-8924)
Wasilla 99654 (865 N. Seward Meridian Parkway, Suite 105, 907-631-3100 or 1-866-323-8648)
Juneau 99802 (Juneau Federal Building, 709 – West 9th Street, Mailing Address: P.O. Box 20069, Juneau, AK 99802, 907-586-7472 or 1-888-308-7890)

Regional Office:
Anchorage 99508-2989 (2925 De Barr Rd., statewide 1-800-827-1000)

Vet Centers:
Anchorage 99508 (4201 Tudor Centre Dr., Suite 115, 907-563-6966)
Fairbanks 99701 (540 4th Ave., Suite 100, 907-456-4238)
Kenai 99669 (Red Diamond Ctr., Bldg. F, Suite 4, 43335 Kalifornsky Beach Rd., 907-260-7640)
Wasilla 99654 (851 E. West Point Dr., Suite 111, 907-376-4318)

National Cemeteries:
Fort Richardson 99505-5498 (Building 997, Davis Hwy., 907-384-7075)
Sitka 99835 (803 Sawmill Creek Rd., 907-384-7075)

AMERICAN SAMOA

Clinics:
Pago Pago 96799 (Fiatele Teo Army Reserve Bldg, Mailing Address: PO Box 1005, Pago Pago, AS 96799, 684-699-3730)

Benefits Office:
Pago Pago 96799 (PO Box 1005, 684-633-5073)

ARIZONA

VA Medical Centers:
Prescott 86313 (500 N. Hwy 89, 928-445-4860 or 800-949-1005)
Tucson 85723 (3601 South 6th Avenue, 520-792-1450 or 800-470-8262)
Phoenix 85012 (650 E. Indian School Rd., 602-277-5551 or 800-554-7174)

Clinics:
Anthem 85086 (Anthem Medical Plaza, 3618 W. Anthem Way, Building D, #120, 623-551-6092)
Bellemont 86015-6196 (P.O. Box 16196, Camp Navajo Army Depot, 928-226-1056)
Buckeye 85326 (306 E. Monroe, 623-386-4814)
Casa Grande 85222 (900 E. Florence Blvd, Suites H & I, 520-629-4900 or 800-470-8262)
Cottonwood 86326 (203 Candy Lane Building 5B, 928-649-1523 or 1532)
Globe 85501 (5860 S. Hospital Dr., Suite 11, 928-425-0027)
Green Valley 85614 (380 W. Hermosa Drive #140, 520-629-4900 or 800-470-8262)
Kingman 86401 (1726 Beverly Ave., 928-692-0080 or 928-445-4860x6830)
Lake Havasu City 86403 (2035 Mesquite, Suite E, 928-680-0090 or 928-445-4860x7300)
Mesa 85212-6033 (6950 E. Williams Field Road, Bldg. 23, 602-222-6568/3315)
Payson 85541 (1106 N. Beeline Highway, 928-472-3148)
Safford 85546 (711 South 14th Ave., 520-629-4900)
Show Low 85901 (2450 Show Low Lake Rd, Suite 1, 928-532-1069)
Sierra Vista 85635 (101 Coronado Dr., Suite A, 520-792-1450)
Sun City 85351 (10147 Grand Ave., Suite C1, 602-222-2630)
Tuscon 85741 (2945 W. Ina Rd., 520-629-4900)
Tuscon 85747 (7395 S. Houghton Rd. Ste. 129, 520-792-1450 or 800-470-8262)
Yuma 85365 (2555 E. Gila Ridge Rd., 520-629-4900)

Regional Office:
Phoenix 85012 (3333 N. Central Ave., statewide 1-800-827-1000)

Vet Centers:
Phoenix 85012 (77 E. Weldon Ave., Suite 100, 602-640-2981)
Phoenix-East Valley 85202 (1303 S. Longmore, Suite 5, Mesa, 480-610-6727)
Prescott 86303 (3180 Stillwater Dr., Suite A, 928-778-3469)
Tucson 85719 (3055 N. 1st Ave., 520-882-0333

National Cemeteries:
Nat. Mem. Cem. of AZ 85024 (23029 N. Cave Creek Rd., Phoenix, 480-513-3600)
Prescott 86301 (500 Hwy. 89 N., 480-513-3600)

ARKANSAS

VA Medical Centers:
Fayetteville 72703 (1100 N. College Ave., 479-443-4301 or 800-691-8387)
Little Rock 72205-5484 (4300 West 7th St., 501-257-1000)
North Little Rock 72114-1706 (2200 Fort Roots Dr., 501-257-1000)

Clinics:
El Dorado 71730 (460 W Oak St, 870-862-2489)
Ft Smith 72917 (1500 Dodson Ave Sparks Medical Plaza, 479-709-6850 or 1-877-604-0798)
Harrison 72601 (707 N Main St., 870-741-3592)
Hot Springs 71913 (1661 Airport Rd, Suite E, 501-881-4112)
Jonesboro 72401 (223 E Jackson, 870-972-0063)
Mena 71953 (1706 Hwy. 71 N, 479-394-4800)
Mountain Home 72653 (#10 Medical Plaza, 870-424-4109)
Mountain Home 72653 (405 Buttercup Dr., 870-425-3030)
Paragould 72450 (1101 Morgan St., 870-236-9756)
Pine Bluff 71603 (4010 Old Warren Road, 870-541-9300)
Texarkana 71854 (910 Realtor Ave., 870-779-2750)

Regional Office:
North Little Rock 72114 (2200 Fort Roots Dr., Bldg. 65, statewide 1-800-827-1000

Vet Center:
North Little Rock 72114 (201 W. Broadway, Suite A, 501-324-6395)

National Cemeteries:
Fayetteville 72701 (700 Government Ave., 479-444-5051)
Fort Smith 72901 (522 Garland Ave., 479-783-5345)
Little Rock 72206 (2523 Confederate Blvd., 501-324-6401)

CALIFORNIA

Regional Offices:
Los Angeles 90024 (Fed. Bldg., 11000 Wilshire Blvd., serving counties of Inyo, Kern, Los Angeles, San Bernardino, San Luis Obispo, Santa Barbara and Ventura, statewide 1-800-827-1000)
Oakland 94612 (1301 Clay St., Rm. 1300 North, serving all CA counties not served by the Los Angeles, San Diego, or Reno VA Regional Offices, 1-800-827-1000)
San Diego 92108 (8810 Rio San Diego Dr., serving Imperial, Orange, Riv-

erside and San Diego, statewide 1-800-827-1000). The counties of Alpine, Lassen, Modoc, and Mono are served by the Reno, NV, Regional Office.

Benefits Office:
Sacramento 95827 (10365 Old Placerville Rd., 916-364-6500)

VA Medical Centers:
Fresno 93703 (2615 E. Clinton Ave., 559-225-6100 or 888-826-2838)
Livermore 94550 (4951 Arroyo Rd., 925-373-4700)
Loma Linda 92357 (11201 Benton St., 909-825-7084 or 800-741-8387)
Long Beach 90822 (5901 E. 7th St., 562-826-8000 or 888-769-8387)
Los Angeles 90073 (11301 Wilshire Blvd., 310-478-3711 or 800-952-4852)
Sacramento 95655 (10535 Hospital Way, Mather, 800-382-8387 or 916-366-5366)
Menlo Park 94025 (795 Willow Rd., 650-416-9997)
Palo Alto 94304-1290 (3801 Miranda Avenue, 650-493-5000 or 800-455-0057)
San Diego 92161 (3350 La Jolla Village Drive, 858-552-8585 or 800-331-8387)
San Francisco 94121-1598 (4150 Clement Street, 415-221-4810 or 800-733-0502)

Clinics:
Anaheim 92801 (Professional Center, 3rd Floor, Suite 303, 1801 W. Romneya Dr., 714-780-5400)
Atwater 95301-5140 (3605 Hospital Road, Suite D, 209-381-0105)
Auburn 95603 (11985 Heritage Oaks Place, 530-889-0872 or 888-227-5404)
Bakersfield 93301 (1801 Westwind Dr., 661-632-1800)
El Centro 92243 (Imperial Valley, 1600 South Imperial Ave., 760-352-1506)
Capitola 95010-3906 (1350 N. 41st St., Suite 102, 831-464-5519)
Chico 95926 (280 Cohasset Rd., 800-382-8387 or 530-879-5000)
Chula Vista 91910 (South Bay, 835 3rd Ave., 619-409-1600)
City of Commerce 90040 (East Los Angeles, 5426 E. Olympic Blvd., 323-725-7557)
Corona 92879 (800 Magnolia Ave., #101, 951-817-8820)
Escondido 92025 (815 E. Pennsylvania Ave., 760-466-7020)
Eureka 95501 (714 F St., 707-442-5335)
Fairfield 94535 (103 Bodin Circle, Travis Air Force Base, 800-382-8387 or 707-437-1800)
Fremont 94538 (39199 Liberty Street, Fremont, 510-791-4000)
French Camp 95231 (Stockton Clinic, 7777 South Freedom Dr., 209-946-3400)
Gardena 90247 (1251 Redondo Beach Blvd, 3rd Floor, 310-851-4705)
Laguna Hills 92653 (25292 McIntyre St., 949-269-0700)
Lancaster 93536 (Antelope Valley, 547 West Lancaster Blvd., 661-729-

8655 or 800-515-0031)
Long Beach 90806 (Villages at Cabrillo: 2001 River Ave, Bldg 28, 562-388-8000)
Los Angeles 90012 (351 East Temple St., 213-253-2677)
Los Angeles 90073 (West Los Angeles Ambulatory Care Center, 11301 Wilshire Blvd., 310-268-3526)
Lynwood 90262 (3737 Martin Luther King Blvd. Suite 515, 310-537-6825)
Martinez 94553 (Clinic and Center for Rehabilitation & Extended Care, 150 Muir Rd., 800-382-8387 or 925-372-2000)
Modesto 95350 (1524 McHenry Ave., 209-557-6200)
Monterey 93955 (3401 Engineer Lane, Seaside, 831-883-3800)
North Hills 91343: (Sepulveda Clinic and Nursing Home, 16111 Plummer St., 818-891-7711 or 800-516-4567)
Oakland 94626 (Mental Health Clinic: 2505 West 14th St., Oakland Army Base, 800-382-8387 or 510-587-3400)
Oakland 94612 (Clinic, 2221 Martin Luther King Jr. Way, 800-382-8387 or 510-267-7800)
Oceanside 92056 (1300 Rancho del Oro Rd.)
Oxnard 93030 (250 W. Citrus Grove Ave., Ste 150, 805-983-6384)
Palm Desert 92211 (41-990 Cook St., Bldg. F, Suite 1004, 951-341-5570)
Rancho Cucamonga 91730 (8599 Haven Ave. 909-946-5348)
Redding 96002 (351 Hartnell Ave., 800-382-8387 or 530-226-7555)
Sacramento 95655 (Mental Health Clinic at Mather, 10633 Grissom Rd., 800-382-8387 or 916-366-5420)
Sacramento 95652 (McClellan Dental Clinic, 5401 Arnold Ave., 800-382-8387 or 916-561-7800)
Sacramento 95652 (McClellan Outpatient Clinic, 5342 Dudley Blvd., 800-382-8387 or 916-561-7400)
San Bruno 94066 (1001 Sneath Lane, Suite 300, Third Floor, 650-615-6000)
San Diego 92108 (Mission Valley, 8810 Rio San Diego Dr., 619-400-5000)
San Francisco 94107 (Downtown Clinic, 401 3rd St., 415-551-7300)
San Gabriel 91776 (Pasadera, 420 W. Las Tunas Drive, 626-289-5973)
San Jose 95119 (80 Great Oaks Boulevard, 408-363-3011)
San Luis Obispo 93401 (Pacific Medical Plaza, 1288 Morro St., Ste.200, 805-543-1233)
Santa Ana 92704 (Bristol Medical Center, 2740 S. Bristol St., 1st Floor, Ste. 101, 714-825-3500)
Santa Barbara 93110 (4440 Calle Real, 805-683-1491)
Santa Fe Springs 90670 (10210 Orr & Day Rd., 562-864-5565)
Santa Maria 93454 (1550 East Main St., 805-354-6000)
Santa Rosa 95404 (3841 Brickway Clvd., 707-569-2300)
Seaside 93955 (Monterey Clinic, 3401 Engineering Lane, 831-883-3800)
Sonora 95370 (19747 Greenley Rd., 209-588-2600)
Stockton 95231 (500 West Hospital Rd., 209-946-3400)
Sun City 92586 (28125 Bradley Road, Suite 130, 951-672-1931)

Susanville 96130 (Diamond View Outpatient Clinic: 110 Bella Way, 775-328-1453) Openning 2010
Tulare 93274 (VA South Valley Clinic, 1050 N. Cherry St., 559-684-8703)
Ukiah 95482 (630 Kings Court 707-468-7700)
Vallejo 94592 (Mare Island Clinic, 201 Walnut Ave., 800-382-8387 or 707-562-8200)
Ventura 93003 (120 N Ashwood Ave., 805-658-5800
Victorville 92395 (12138 Industrial Boulevard, Suite 120, 760-951-2599)

Regional Offices:
Los Angeles 90024 (Fed. Bldg., 11000 Wilshire Blvd., serving counties of Inyo, Kern, Los Angeles, San Bernardino, San Luis Obispo, Santa Barbara and Ventura, statewide 1-800-827-1000)
Oakland 94612 (1301 Clay St., Rm. 1300 North, serving all CA counties not served by the Los Angeles, San Diego, or Reno VA Regional Offices, 1-800-827-1000)
San Diego 92108 (8810 Rio San Diego Dr., serving Imperial, Orange, Riverside and San Diego, statewide 1-800-827-1000). The counties of Alpine, Lassen, Modoc, and Mono are served by the Reno, NV, Regional Office.

Benefits Office:
Sacramento 95827 (10365 Old Placerville Rd., 916-364-6500)

Vet Centers:
Anaheim 92805 (859 S. Harbor Blvd., 714-776-0161)
Colton 92324(11325 E. Cooley Dr., Suite 101, 909-801-5762)
Chico 95926 (280 Cohasset Rd., Suite 100, 530-899-8549)
Concord 94520 (1899 Clayton Rd., Suite 140, 925-680-4526)
Corona 92879 (800 Magnolia Ave., 110, 951-734-0525)
East Los Angeles 90022 (5400 E. Olympic Blvd., 140, 323-728-9966)
Eureka 95501 (2830 G St., Suite A, 707-444-8271)
Fresno 93726 (3636 N. 1st St., Suite 112, 559-487-5660)
Gardena 90247 (1045 W. Redondo Beach Blvd., 150, Gardena, 310-767-1221)
West Los Angeles 90230 (5730 Uplander Way, Suite 100, Culver City, 310-641-0326)
Modesto 95351 (1219 N. Carpenter Rd., Suites 11 & 12, 209-527-1359 or 209-527-5961)
Oakland 94612 (1504 Franklin St., 200, 510-763-3904)
Redwood City 94062 (2946 Broadway St., 650-299-0672)
Rohnert Park 94928 (6225 State Farm Dr., Suite 101, 707-586-3295)
Sacramento 95825 (1111 Howe Ave., Suite 390, 916-566-7430)
San Diego 92103 (2790 Truxton Rd. Suite 130, 858-642-1500)
San Francisco 94102 (505 Polk St., 415-441-5051)
San Jose 95112 (278 N. 2nd St., 408-993-0729)

San Marcos 92069 (1 Civic Center Dr., Suite 150, 760-744-6914)
Santa Cruz 95010 (1350 41st Ave., Suite 102, 831-464-4575)
Sepulveda 91343 (9737 Haskell Ave., 818-892-9227)
Temecula 92591 (40935 County Center Dr. Suite A&B 951-296-5608
Ventura 93001 (790 E. Santa Clara, Suite 100, 805-585-1860)
Victorville 92394 (15095 Amargosa Rd. Suite 107, 760-955-9703)

National Cemeteries:
Bakersfield 93301 (30338 E. Bear Mountain Blvd., Bakersfield, 866-632-1845)
Fort Rosecrans 92106 (P.O. Box 6237, Point Loma, San Diego, 619-553-2084)
Golden Gate 94066 (1300 Sneath Ln., San Bruno, 650-589-7737)
Los Angeles 90049 (950 South Sepulveda Blvd., 310-268-4675)
Riverside 92518 (22495 Van Buren Blvd., 951-653-8417)
Sacramento Valley VA 95620 (5810 Midway Rd., Dixon, 707-693-2460)
San Francisco 94129 (1 Lincoln Blvd., Presidio of San Francisco, 650-589-7737)
San Joaquin Valley 95322 (32053 West McCabe Rd., Santa Nella, 209-854-1040)

COLORADO

Medical Centers:
Denver 80220 (1055 Clermont Street, 303-399-8020 or toll free: 888-336-8262)
Grand Junction 81501 (2121 North Avenue, 970-263-2800 or toll free 866-206-6415)
Health Administration Center:
Denver 80209 (3773 Cherry Creek North Dr., 303-331-7500)

Clinics:
Alamosa 81101 (San Luis Valley Clinic/Sierra Blanca Med. Ctr.: 622 Del Sol Drive, 719-587-6800 or toll free 1-866-659-0930)
Aurora 80045 (13001 East 17th Place, Bld. 500, 2nd Floor, West Wing, 303-724-0190)
Burlington 80807 (1177 Rose Avenue, 719-346-5239)
Colorado Springs 80905 (25 North Spruce St., 719-327-5660 or toll free 800-278-3883)
Craig 81625 (551 Tucker Street, 970-824-9721 or 970-242-0731)
Durango 81301 (400 S. Camino Del Rio, 970-247-2214)
Fort Collins 80526 (2509 Research Blvd. 970-224-1550 Or 888-481-8828)
Greeley 80631 (2001 70th Ave Suite# 200 970-313-0027 Or 888-481-4065
La Junta 81050 (1100 Carson Ave., Suite 104, 719-383-5195)
Lakewood 80225 (155 Van Gordon St., Suite 395, 303-914-2680)
Lamar 81052 (High Plains Community Health Center 201 Kendall Dr., 719-336-5972)

Montrose 81401 (4 Hillcrest Plaza Way, 970-249-7791 or 970-242-0731)
Pueblo 81008 (4112 Outlook Boulevard, 719-553-1000 or 800-369-6748)
Salida 81201 (920 Rush Drive, 719-539-8666)

Regional Office:
Denver 80225 (Mailing Address: PO Box 25126. Physical Address: 155 Van
Gordon St., Lakewood, 80228, statewide 1-800-827-1000)

Vet Centers:
Boulder 80302 (2336 Canyon Blvd., Suite 103, 303-440-7306)
Colorado Springs 80903 (602 N. Nevada Ave., 719-471-9992)
Denver 80230 (7465 E. First Ave., Ste. B, 303-326-0645)
Grand Junction 81505 (2472 F. Rd. Unit 16, 970-245-4156)

National Cemeteries:
Fort Logan 80236 (4400 W. Kenyon Ave., Denver, 303-761-0117)
Fort Lyon 81504 (15700 County Road HH, Las Animas, 303-761-0117)

CONNECTICUT
VA Medical Centers:
Newington 06111 (555 Willard Ave., 860-666-6951)
West Haven 06516 (950 Campbell Avenue, 203-932-5711)

Clinics:
Danbury 06810 (7 Germantown Rd., Suite 2B, 203-798-8422)
New London 06320 (Shaw's Cove Four, 860-437-3611)
Stamford 06905 (1275 Summer St, Suite 102, 203-325-0649)
Waterbury 06706 (95 Scovill St., 203-465-5292)
Windham 06226 (Windham Hospital, 96 Mansfield St., 860-450-7583)
Winsted 06908 (Winsted Health Center, 115 Spencer St., 860-738-6985)

Regional Office:
Hartford (Bldg 2E – RM 5137, 555 Willard Ave.; Newington, 06111-2693,
statewide 1-800-827-1000)

Vet Centers:
Wethersfield 06109 (30 Jordan Lane, 860-563-2320)
Rocky Hill 06067 (25 Elm St. 860-563-8800
Norwich 06360 (2 Cliff St., 860-887-1755)
West Haven 06516 (141 Captain Thomas Blvd., 203-932-9899)

DELAWARE
VA Medical Center:
Wilmington 19805 (1601 Kirkwood Highway, 302-994-2511 or
800-461-8262)

Clinics:
Dover 19901 (1198 Governors Ave., 302-994-2511 x2400)
Georgetown 19947 (15 Georgetown Plaza, 302-994-2511 x5251

Regional Office:
Wilmington 19805 (1601 Kirkwood Hwy., local, 302-994-2511)
Vet Center:
Wilmington 19805 (2710 Centerville Rd. Suite 103, 302-994-1660)

DISTRICT OF COLUMBIA

VA Medical Center:
Washington 20422 (50 Irving Street, NW, 202-745-8000 or 888-553-0242)

Clinic:
Washington 20032 (820 Chesapeake Street, S.E., 202-745-8685)

Regional Office:
Washington, D.C., 20421 (1722 I St., N.W., local, 1-800-827-1000)
Vet Center:
Washington, D.C. 20011 (1250 Taylor St., N.W., 202-726-5212)

FLORIDA

VA Medical Centers:
Bay Pines 33744 (10000 Bay Pines Blvd., P.O. Box 5005, Bay Pines, FL
   33744, 727-398-6661/888-820-0230)
Gainesville 32608-1197 (1601 S.W. Archer Rd., 352-376-1611 or 800-324-
   8387)
Lake City 32025-5808 (619 S. Marion Avenue, 386-755-3016 or 800-308-
   8387)
Miami 33125 (1201 N.W. 16th St., 305-575-7000 or 888-276-1785)
Orlando 32803 (5201 Raymond St., 407-629-1599 or 800-922-7521)
Tampa 33612 (13000 Bruce B. Downs Blvd., 813-972-2000 or 888-716-
   7787)
West Palm Beach 33410-6400 (7305 N. Military Trail, 561-422-8262 or
   800-972-8262)
Clinics:
Boca Raton 33433 (901 Meadows Rd., 561-416-8995)
Bradenton (5530 S.R. 64, Bradenton, FL 34208)
Brooksville 34613 (14540 Cortez Blvd., Suite 200, 352-597-8287)
Broward 33351 (9800 West Commercial Blvd., 954-745-5500)
Coral Springs 33065 (9900 West Sample Road, Suite 100, 954-575-4940)
Daytona Beach 32114 (551 National Health Care Dr., 386-323-7500)
Deerfield Beach 33442 (2100 S.W. 10th St., 954-570-5572)
Delray Beach 33445 (4800 Linton Blvd., Suite 300E, 561-495-1973)
Eglin AFB 32542 (100 Veterans Way, 850-609-2600/866-520-7359)
Fort Myers 33916 (3033 Winkler Extension, 239-939-3939)

Ft. Pierce 34950 (727 North US 1, 772-595-5150)
Hollywood 33021 (3702 Washington St., Suite 201, 954-986-1811)
Hollywood 33024 (Pembroke Pines, 7369 W. Sheridan St., Suite 102, 954-894-1668)
Homestead 33030 (950 Krome Avenue, Suite 401, 305-248-0874)
Jacksonville 32206 (1833 Boulevard, 904-232-2751)
Key Largo 33037 (105662 Overseas Highway, 305-451-0164)
Key West 33040 (1300 Douglas Circle, Building L-15, 305-293-4609)
Kissimmee 34741 (2285 North Central Avenue, 407-518-5004)
Lakeland 33803 (3240 S. Florida Avenue, 863-701-2470)
Lecanto 34461 (2804 W. Marc Knighton Ct., Suite A, 352-746-8000)
Leesburg 34748 (711 W. Main St., 352-435-4000)
Marianna 32446 (4970 Highway 90, 850-718-5620)
Miami 33135 (Healthcare for Homeless Veterans, 1492 West Flagler St., 305-541-5864)
Miami 33135 (Substance Abuse Clinic, 1492 West Flagler St., Suite 101, 305-541-8435)
Naples 34104 (2685 Horseshoe Drive - Suite 101, 239-659-9188)
New Port Richey 34654 (9912 Little Road, 727-869-4100)
Ocala 34470 (1515 Silver Springs Blvd., 352-369-3320)
Okeechobee 34972 (1201 N. Parrot Avenue, 863-824-3232)
Orange City 32763 (2583 South Volusia Ave., Ste 300, 386-456-2080)
Palm Harbor (35209 US Highway 19 North 727-734-5276)
Panama City Clinic 32407 (101 Vernon Ave, Building 387, 850-636-7000/888-231-5047)
Panama City Mental Health 32408 (4408 Delwood Ln, 850-636-7000/888-231-5047)
Panama City Beach 32407 (6703 West Highway 98, 850-636-7000)
Panama City Beach 32407-7018 (Naval Support Activity-Panama City, 101 Vernon Ave #387, 850-636-7000)
Pembroke Pines (Pembroke Pines, 7369 W. Sheridan St., Suite 102, 954-894-1668)
Pensacola 32507 (Joint Ambulatory Care Center, 790 Veterans Way, 850-912-2000/866-927-1420)
Pensacola 32503 (312 Kenmore Road, 850-476-1100)
St. Petersburg (840 Dr. MLK Street North 727-502-1700)
Port Charlotte 33952 (4161 Tamiami Trail, 941-235-2710)
Port St. Lucie County PTSD Clinic 34986 (126 SW Chambers Court 772878-7876)
Sanford 32771 (1403 Medical Plaza Drive, Suite 109, 407-323-5999)
Sarasota 34233 (5682 Bee Ridge Rd., Suite 100, 941-371-3349)
Sebring 33870 (3760 U.S. Highway 27 South, 863-471-6227, Mental Health Phone 863-314-0325)
St. Augustine 32086 (1955 U.S. 1 South, Suite 200, 904-829-0814 or 866-401-8387)
Stuart 34997 (3501 S E Willoughby Boulevard, 772-288-0304)

Sunrise 33351 (9800 W Commercial St., 954-475-5500)
Tallahassee 32308 (1607 St. James Ct., 850-878-0191)
The Villages 32162 (Laurel Lake Professional Park, 1950 Laurel Manor
  Drive, Building 240, 352-205-8900)
Vero Beach 32960 (372 17th Street, 772-299-4623)
Viera 32940 (2900 Veterans Way 321-637-3788)
Zephyrhills 33541 (6937 Medical View Ln., 813-780-2550)

Regional Office:
St. Petersburg 33708 (mailing address: P.O. Box 1437, 33731; physical
  address: 9500 Bay Pines Blvd., statewide 1-800-827-1000)
Benefits Offices:
Fort Lauderdale 33301 (VR&E-28S, 9800 W. Commercial Blvd., Sunrise,
  FL 33351 1-800-827-1000)
Jacksonville 32256 (VR&E, 7825 Baymeadows Way, Suite 120-B, 1-800-
  827-1000)
Orlando 32801 (1000 Legion Pl., VRE-Suite 1500, C&P-Suite 1550, 1-800-
  827-1000)
Pensacola 32503-7492 (C&P, 312 Kenmore Rd., Rm. 1G250, 1-800-827-
  1000)
West Palm Beach 33410 (C&P, 7305 North Military Tr., Suite 1A-167,
  1-800-827-1000)

Vet Centers:
Clearwater 33761 (29298 US Highway 19N., 727-549-3600)
Ft. Lauderdale 33304 (713 N.E. 3rd Ave., 954-356-7926)
Fort Myers 33916 (4110 Center Pointe Drive, Unit 204, 239-479-4401)
Gainesville 32607 (105 NW 75th St., Suite 2, 352-331-1408)
Jacksonville 32202 (300 East State St., 904-232-3621)
Jupiter 33458 (2074 W, Indiantown Road, Suite 100, 561-422-1220)
Melbourne 32935 (2098 Sarno Rd., 321-254-3410)
Miami 33122 (8280 NW 27th St., Suite 511, 305-859-8387)
Orlando 32822 (5575 S. Semoran Blvd., Suite 36, 407-857-2800)
Palm Beach 33461 (2311 10th Ave., North 13, 561-585-0441)
Pensacola 32501 (4501 Twin Oaks Dr., 850-456-5886)
Sarasota 34231 (4801 Swift Rd., 941-927-8285)
St. Petersburg 33710 (6798 Crosswinds Drive, Building A, 727-549-3633)
Tallahassee 32303 (548 Bradford Rd., 850-942-8810)
Tampa 33614 (3637 W. Waters Avenue, Suite 600, 813-228-2621)

National Cemeteries:
Barrancas 32508-1054 (80 Hovey Rd., Naval Air Station, Pensacola, 850-
  453-4846)
Bay Pines 33504-0477 (10000 Bay Pines Blvd., Bay Pines, 727-398-9426)
Florida 33513 (6502 SW 102nd Ave., Bushnell, 352-793-7740)
Jacksonville 32218 (4083 Lannie Rd., 904-766-5222)
St. Augustine 32084 (104 Marine St., 352-793-7740)

South Florida 33467 (6501 South State Road 7, Lake Worth, 561-649-6489)
Sarasota 34241 (9810 State Road 72, Sarasota, 941-922-7200)

GEORGIA
VA Medical Centers:
Augusta 30904-6285 (1 Freedom Way, 706-733-0188 or 800-836-5561)
Decatur 30033 (1670 Clairmont Road, 404-321-6111 or 800-944-9726)
Dublin 31021 (1826 Veterans Blvd., 478-272-1210 or 800-595-5229)

Clinics:
Albany 31701 (526 West Broad Avenue 229-446-9000)
Athens 30601 (9249 Highway 29, 706-227-4534)
Columbus 31906 (1310 13th St., 706-257-7200)
Decatur 30030 (755 Commerce Dr., 2nd Floor, 404-417-5200)
East Point 30344 (1513 Cleveland Ave., 404-321-6111 x2600)
Kathleen 31047 (2370 S. Houston Lake Rd., 478-224-1309)
Lawrenceville 30043 (1970 Riverside Pkwy, 404-417-1750)
Macon 31220 (5398 Thomaston Road, Suite B, 478-476-8868)
Newnan 30265 (39-A Oak Hill, 404-329-222
Oakwood 30566 (3931 Munday Mill Rd., 404-728-8212)
Perry Outreach (2370 S. Houston Lake Road, 478-224-1309)
Rome 30161 (30 Chateau Dr, SE, 706-235-6581)
Savannah 31406 (325 West Montgomery Crossroads, 912-920-0214)
Smyrna 30082 (562 Concord Road, 404-417-1760)
St. Marys 31558 (205 Lake Shore Point, 912-510-3420)
Stockbridge 30281 (175 Medical Blvd., 404-329-2222)
Valdosta 31602 (2841 N. Patterson Street, 229-293-0132)

Regional Office:
Decatur 30033 (1700 Clairmont Rd., statewide 1-800-827-1000)

Vet Centers:
Atlanta 30324 (1440 Dutch Valley Place, Suite 1100, 404-347-7264)
Lawrenceville 30043 (930 River Centre Place, 404-728-4195)
Macon 31201 (750 Riverside Dr., 478-477-3813)
Marietta 30060 (40 Dodd Street, Suite 700, 404-327-4954)
Savannah 31406 (321 Commercial Drive, 912-961-5800)

National Cemeteries:
Georgia 30114 (2025 Mt. Carmel Church Lane, Canton, 866-236-8159)
Marietta 30060 (500 Washington Ave., 866-236-8159)

GUAM
Clinic:
Agana Heights 96919 (U.S. Naval Hospital, Bldg-1, E-200, Box 7608, 671-344-9200)

Benefits Office/Vet Center:
Hagatna 96910 (Reflection Center, Suite 201, 222 Chalan Santo Papa St.,
671-472-7161)

HAWAII

Medical Center:
Honolulu 96819-1522 (459 Patterson Rd., E Wing) (toll-free from Hawaii,
Guam, Saipan, Rota and Tinian at 1-800-827-1000; toll-free from American
Samoa at 1-877-899-4400)

Clinics:
Hilo 96720 (1285 Wainuenue Ave., Suite 211, 808-935-3781)
Honolulu PTSD 96819 (3375 Koapaka St.,Suite I-560, 808-566-1546)
Kauai; Lihue 96766 (3-3367 Kuhio Hwy., Suite 200, 808-246-0497)
Kona; Kailua-Kona 75-377 Hualalai Rd., Kailua-Kona 808-329-0774
Maui; Kahului 96732 (203 Ho'ohana St., Suite 303, 808-871-2454)

Regional Office:
Honolulu 96819-1522 (459 Patterson Rd., E Wing. Mailing address: PO
Box 29020, Honolulu, HI 96820) (toll-free from Hawaii, Guam, Saipan,
Rota and Tinian, 1-800-827-1000; toll-free from American Samoa, 1-877-
899-4400)
VR&E Benefits Offices:
Hilo 96720 (1285 Waianuenue, 2nd Floor, 808-935-6691)
Kahului 96732 (203 Ho'ohana St., 808-873-9426)

Vet Centers:
Hilo 96720 (126 Pu'uhonu,Way, Suite 2, Hilo 808-969-3833)
Honolulu 96814 (1680 Kapiolani Blvd., Suite F.3, 808-973-8387)
Kailua-Kona 96740 96740 (Hale Kui Plaza, Suite 207, 73-4976 Kamanu
St., 808-329-0574)
Lihue 96766 (3-3367 Kuhio Hwy., Suite 101, 808-246-1163)
Wailuku 96793 (35 Lunalilo, Suite 101, 808-242-8557)
National Cemetery:
Nat. Cem. of the Pacific 96813-1729 (2177 Puowaina Dr., Honolulu, 808-
532-3720)

IDAHO

Medical Center:
Boise 83702 (500 West Fort St., 208-422-1000)

Clinics:
Caldwell 83605 (120 E. Pine St., 208-454-4820)
Coeur d'Alene 83815 (2177 N. Ironwood Dr. 208-665-1700)
Lewiston 83501 (1630 23rd Ave., Stes. 301 & 401, Bldg. 2, 208-746-7784)
Pocatello 83201 (444 Hospital Way, Suite 801, 208-232-6214)
Salmon 83467 (111 Lillian St., #203, 208-756-8515)

Twin Falls 83301 (260 2nd Ave, E., 208-732-0947)

Regional Office:
Boise 83702 (444 W. Fort St., statewide, 1-800-827-1000)

Vet Centers:
Boise 83705 (2424 Bank Drive, 208-342-3612)
Pocatello 83201 (1800 Garrett Way, 208-232-0316)

ILLINOIS
VA Medical Centers:
Aurora 60504 (750 Shoreline Drive, Suite 150, 708-516-7529
Chicago 60612 (820 South Damen Ave., 312-569-8387)
Danville 61832-5198 (1900 East Main Street, 217-554-3000 or 800-320-8387)
Hines 60141 (5000 S 5th Ave., 708-202-8387)
Marion 62959 (2401 West Main, 618-997-5311)
North Chicago 60064 (3001 Green Bay Road, 847-688-1900 or 800-393-0865)

Clinics:
Aurora 60506 (1700 N. Landmark Road, 630-859-2504)
Belleville 62223 (6500 W Main St., 314-286-6988)
Chicago 60620 (7731 S Halsted St., 773-962-3700)
Chicago 60611 (211 E. Ontario, 312-569-8387)
Chicago Heights 60411 (30 E. 15th Street, Suite 207, 708-756-5454)
Decatur 62526-9381 (3035 East Mound Road, 217-875-2670)
Effingham 62401 (1901 S 4th St Suite 21, 217-347-7600)
Elgin 60120 (450 W. Dundee Rd., 847-742-5920)
Evanston 60202 (107 - 109 Clyde St., 847-869-6315)
Freeport 61032 (1301 Kiwanis Dr., 815-235-4881)
Galesburg 61401 (387 East Grove, 309-343-0311)
Joliet 60435 (2000 Glenwood Ave., 815-744-0492)
LaSalle 61301 (2970 Chartres, 815-223-9678)
Manteno 60950 (Illinois Veterans Home, One Veterans Dr., 815-468-1027)
Mattoon (501 Lake Land Blvd. 217-258-3370)
McHenry 60050 (620 South Route 31, 815-759-2306)
Mt. Vernon 62864 (1 Doctors Park Rd., 618-246-2910)
Oak Lawn 60453 (4700 W. 95th St., 708-499-3675)
Oak Park 60302 (149 S. Oak Park Ave., 708-386-3008)
Orland Park 60462 (8651 W. 159th Street, 708-444-0561)
Peoria 61605-2400 (411 Dr. Martin Luther King Jr. Dr., 309-497-0790)
Quincy 62301 (721 Broadway, 217-224-3366)
Rockford 61108 (4940 East State St., 815-227-0081)
Rockford 61108 (4960 E. State Street, Bldg 3, 815-395-1276)
Springfield 62702 (700 North 7th Street, Suite C, 217-522-9730)

Regional Office:
Chicago 60612 (2122 W. Taylor St., statewide 1-800-827-1000)

Vet Centers:
Chicago 60620 (7731 S. Halsted St., Suite 200, 773-962-3740)
Chicago Heights 60411 (1600 S. Halsted St., 708-754-0340)
East St. Louis 62203 (1265 N. 89th St., Suite 5, 618-397-6602)
Evanston 60202 (565 Howard St., 847-332-1019)
Moline 61265 (1529 46th Ave., 6, 309-762-6954)
Oak Park 60302 (155 S. Oak Park Blvd., 708-383-3225)
Peoria 61603 (3310 N. Prospect Rd., 309-671-7300)
Springfield 62702 (624 S. 4th St., 217-492-4955)

National Cemeteries:
Abraham Lincoln 60421 (20953 W. Hoff Rd., Elwood, 815-423-9958)
Alton 62003 (600 Pearl St., 314-845-8320)
Camp Butler 62707 (5063 Camp Butler Rd., Springfield, 217-492-4070)
Danville 61832 (1900 East Main St., 217-554-4550)
Mound City 62963 (Junction Highways 37 & 51, 314-845-8320)
Quincy 62301 (36th and Maine St., 309-782-2094)
Rock Island 61299-7090 (Rock Island Arsenal, Bldg. 118, 309-782-2094)

INDIANA
VA Medical Centers:
Fort Wayne 46805 (2121 Lake Ave., 260-426-5431 or 800-360-8387)
Indianapolis 46202 (1481 W. 10th St., 317-554-0000 or 888-878-6889)
Marion 46953-4589 (1700 East 38th St., 765-674-3321 or 800-360-8387)
Muncie 47303-5263 (2600 W. White River Blvd., 765-284-6822)

Clinics:
Bloomington 47403 (455 South Landmark Avenue, 812-336-5723, or toll
   free 877-683-0865)
Crown Point 46307 (9330 S. Broadway, 219-662-5000)
Evansville 47713 (500 E Walnut St., 812-465-6202)
Goshen 46526 (2014 Lincolnway East Ste. #3, 574-534-6108)
Greendale 47025 (1600 Flossie Dr., 812-539-2313)
Muncie 47304-6357 (3500 W. Purdue Ave., 765-284-6822)
New Albany 47150 (811 Northgate Blvd, 502-287-4100)
Richmond 47374 (4351 South A St., 765-973-6915)
Scottsburg 47170 (279 N. Gardner, St., 812-752-8375)
South Bend 46614-9668 (5735 S. Ironwood Road, 574-299-4847)
Terre Haute 47802 (110 W Honeycreek Pkwy, 812-232-2890)
Vincennes 47591 (1813 Willow St. Ste. 6A, 812-882-0894)
West Lafayette 47906 (3851 N. River Road, 765-464-2280)

Regional Office:
Indianapolis 46204 (575 N. Pennsylvania St., statewide 1-800-827-1000)

Vet Centers:
Evansville 47711 (311 N. Weinbach Ave., 812-473-5993)
Fort Wayne 46802 (528 West Berry St., 260-460-1456)
Merrillville 46410 (6505 Broadway Ave., 219-736-5633)
Indianapolis 46208 (3833 N. Meridian St., Suite 120, 317-927-1600)

National Cemeteries:
Crown Hill 46208 (700 W. 38th St., Indianapolis, 765-674-0284)
Marion 46952 (1700 E. 38th St., 765-674-0284)
New Albany 47150 (1943 Ekin Ave., 502-893-3852)

IOWA
VA Medical Centers:
Des Moines 50310-5774 (3600 30th St., 515-699-5999 or 800-294-8387)
Iowa City 52246-2208 (601 Highway 6 West, 319-338-0581 or 800-637-0128)
Knoxville 50138 (1515 W. Pleasant Street, 641-842-3101 or 800-816-8878)

Clinics:
Bettendorf 52722 (2979 Victoria St., 563-332-8528)
Dubuque 52001 (Mercy Health Center, 250 Mercy Dr., 563-589-8899)
Fort Dodge 50501 (2419 2nd Avenue N, 515-576-2235)
Mason City 50401 (520 S. Pierce, Suite 150, 641-421-8077)
Shenandoah 51601 (512 S. Fremont St, 712-246-0092)
Sioux City 51104 (1551 Indian Hills Drive, Suite 206, 712-258-4700)
Spirit Lake 51360 (1310 Lake St., 712-336-6400)
Waterloo 50701 (1015 S Hackett Rd., 319-235-1230)

Regional Office:
Des Moines 50309 (210 Walnut St., Rm. 1063, statewide 1-800-827-1000)

Vet Centers:
Cedar Rapids 52402 (1642 42nd St. N.E., 319-378-0016)
Des Moines 50310 (2600 Martin Luther King Jr. Pkwy., 515-284-4929)
Sioux City 51104 (1551 Indian Hills Dr., Suite 214, 712-255-3808)
National Cemetery:
Keokuk 52632 (1701 J St., 309-782-2094)
National Cemetery:
Keokuk 52632 (1701 J St., 309-782-2094)

KANSAS
VA Medical Centers:
Leavenworth 66048-5055 (150 Muncie Rd., 913-682-2000 or 800-952-

8387)
Topeka 66622 (2200 SW, Gage Boulevard, 785-350-3111 or 800-574-8387)
Wichita 67218 (5500 E. Kellogg, 316-685-2221 or 888-878-6881)

Clinics:
Chanute 66720 (629 South Plummer, 1-800-574-8387 Ext. 54453)
Emporia 66801 (Newman Hospital, 919 W. 12th Avenue, Suite D, 1-800-574-8387 Ext. 54453)
Ft. Dodge 67801 (300 Custer, 1-888-878-6881 x41040)
Ft. Scott 66701 (902 Horton St., 620-223-8655)
Garnett 66032 (Anderson County Hospital: 421 South Maple, 1-800-574-8387 Ext. 54453)
Hays 67601 (Hays Clinic: 207-B East Seventh, 1-888-878-6881 x41000)
Holton 66436 (Holton Community Hospital: 1110 Columbine Dr., 1-800-574-8387 Ext. 54453)
Hutchinson 67502 (1625 E. 30th Ave., 888-878-6881 x41100)
Junction City 66441 (715 Southwind Dr., 800-574-8387 ext. 54670)
Kansas City 66102 21 N 12th Street, Bethany Medical Building, Suite 110, 1-800-952-8387 ext. 56990)
Lawrence 66049 (2200 Harvard Road, 800-574-8387 ext. 54650)
Liberal 67901 (Liberal Clinic: 2 Rock Island Road, Suite 200, 620-626-5574)
Paola 66071 (510 South Hospital Drive, 816-922-2160)
Manhattan Vet Center, 205 S. 4th St. Suite 1B, Manhattan, KS 66502
Parsons 67357 (1907 Harding Drive, 1-888-878-6881 x41060)
Russell 67665 (Regional Hospital Medical Arts Building: 200 South Main St., 785-483-3131 ext. 155)
Salina 67401 (1410 E. Iron, Suite 1, 1-888-878-6881 x41020)
Seneca 66538 (Nemaha Valley Community Hospital: 1600 Community Dr., 1-800-574-8387 EXT 54453)

Regional Office:
Wichita 67208 (Wichita Regional Office, P.O. Box 21318, 1-800-827-1000)

Vet Center:
Wichita 67202 (251 N. Water, 316-685-2221, ext 41080)

National Cemeteries:
Fort Leavenworth 66027 (395 Biddle Blvd., 913-758-4105)
Fort Scott 66701 (900 East National Ave., 620-223-2840)
Leavenworth 66048 (4101 South 4th St., Traffic Way, 913-758-4105)

KENTUCKY
VA Medical Centers:
Lexington-Cooper Division 40502 (1101 Veterans Dr., 859-233-4511 or

888-824-3577)
Lexington-Leestown Division 40511 (2250 Leestown Rd., 859-233-4511 or 888-824-3577)
Louisville 40206 (800 Zorn Avenue, 502-287-4000 or 800-376-8387)

Clinics:
Bellevue 41073 (103 Landmark Dr., 859-392-3840)
Berea (209 Pauline Drive 859-986-1259)
Bowling Green 42103 (Hartland Medical Plaza, 1110 Wilkinson Trace Cir., 270-796-3590)
Carrollton 41008 (309 Eleventh St., 502-732-7146)
Clarkson 42726 (Grayson County, 619 W. Main St., 866-653-8232)
Florence 41042 (7711 Ewing, 859-282-4480)
Ft. Campbell 42223 (Desert Storm Ave. Building 39, 270-798-4118)
Ft Knox 40121 (851 Ireland Loop, 502-624-9396)
Hanson 42413 (926 Veterans Drive, 270-322-8019)
Hazard 41701 (210 Black Gold Blvd., 606-436-2350)
Hopkinsville (1102 South Virginia Drive 270-885-2106)
Louisville 40207 (4010 Dupont Circle, 502-287-6986)
Louisville-Newburg 40218 (3430 Newburg Rd., 502-287-6223)
Louisville-Shively 40216 (3934 North Dixie Highway, Suite 210, 502-287-6000)
Louisville-Standiford Field 40213 (1101 Grade Ln., 502-413-4635)
Mayfield 42066 (1253 Paris Rd Suite A, 270-247-2455)
Morehead (333 Beacon Hill Drive, Suite 100 (606) 784-3004) Owensboro 42301 (3400 New Hartford Rd., 270-684-5034)
Owensboro 42303 (3400 New Hartford Road, 270-684-5034)
Paducah 42001 (2620 Perkins Creek Dr., 270-444-8465)
Prestonsburg 41653 (5230 Ky. Route 321, Suite 8)
Somerset 42503 (104 Hardin Ln., 606-676-0786)

Regional Office:
Louisville 40202 (321 W. Main St., Ste., 390, statewide 1-800-827-1000)

Vet Centers:
Lexington 40507 (301 E. Vine St., Suite C, 859-253-0717)
Louisville 40208 (1347 S. 3rd St., 502-634-1916)

National Cemeteries:
Camp Nelson 40356 (6980 Danville Rd., Nicholasville, 859-885-5727)
Cave Hill 40204 (701 Baxter Ave., Louisville, 502-893-3852)
Danville 40442 (277 N. First St., 859-885-5727)
Lebanon 40033 (20 Highway 208, 502-893-3852)
Lexington 40508 (833 W. Main St., 859-885-5727)
Mill Springs 42544 (9044 West Highway 80, Nancy, 859-885-5727)
Zachary Taylor 40207 (4701 Brownsboro Rd., Louisville, 502-893-3852)

LOUISIANA

VA Medical Centers:
New Orleans 70113 (1250 Poydras St., Suite 200., 1-800-827-1000)
Alexandria 71306 (P. O. Box 69004, 318-473-0010 or 800-375-8387)
Shreveport 71101-4295 (510 E. Stoner Ave., 318-221-8411 or 800-863-7441)

Clinics:
Baton Rouge 70809 (7968 Essen Park Ave., 225-761-3400)
Hammond 70403 (1131 South Morrison Ave., 985-902-5026)
Houma 70360 (1750 Martin Luther King Jr Blvd Ste 107, 985-851-0188)
Jennings 70546 (1907 Johnson St., 337-824-1000)
Lafayette 70501 (2100 Jefferson St., 337-261-0734)
Monroe 71203 (250 De Siard Plaza Dr., 318-343-6100)
Reserve 70084 (247 Veterans Blvd., 504-565-4705)
Slidell 70461 (340 Gateway Dr., 1-800-935-8387)

Regional Office:
New Orleans 70113 (1250 Poydras St., Suite 200., 1-800-827-1000)

Vet Centers:
Baton Rouge 70809 (5207 Essen Lane, Suite 2, 225-757-0045)
New Orleans 70062 (2200 Veterans Memorial Blvd., Suite 114, 504-565-4977)
Kenner 70062 (2200 Veterans Blvd., Suite 114, 504-464-4743)
Shreveport 71104 (2800 Youree Dr., Bldg. 1, Suite 1, 318-861-1776)

National Cemeteries:
Alexandria 71360 (209 E. Shamrock St., Pineville, 601-445-4981)
Baton Rouge 70806 (220 N. 19th St., 225-654-3767)
Port Hudson 70791 (20978 Port Hickey Rd., Zachary, 225-654-3767)

MAINE

VA Medical Center:
Augusta 04330 (1 VA Center, 207-623-8411 or 877-421-8263)

Clinics:
Bangor 04401 304 Hancock St., Suite 3B, 207-561-3600)
Calais 04619 (50 Union St., 207-904-3700)
Caribou 04736   (163 Van Buren Drive, Suite 6, 207-493-3800)
Lincoln 04457 (99 River Road, 207-403-2000)
Rumford 04726 (431 Franklin St., 207-369-3200)
Saco 04072 (655 Main St., 207-294-3100)

Regional Office:
Togus 04330 (One VA Center, Augusta, statewide 1-800-827-1000; VR&E

Division 207-623-8411 ext 4600)

Vet Centers:
Bangor 04401 (368 Harlow St., 207-947-3391)
Caribou 04619 (456 York St., York Street Complex, 207-496-3900)
Lewiston 04240 (Pkwy Complex, 29 Westminster St., 207-783-0068)
Portland 04103 (475 Stevens Ave., 207-780-3584)
Springvale 04083 (628 Main St., 207-490-1513)
National Cemetery:
Togus NC 04330 (1 VA Center; 508-563-7113/4)

MARYLAND
Regional Office:
Baltimore 21201 (Federal Building, 31 Hopkins Plaza, 1-800-827-1000)

VA Medical Centers:
Baltimore 21201 (10 North Greene St., 410-605-7000 or 800-463-6295)
Baltimore-Rehabilitation and Extended Care Center 21218 (3900 Loch
Raven Boulevard, 410-605-7000 or 800-463-6295)
Perry Point 21902 (410-642-2411 or 800 949-1003)

Clinics:
Baltimore-Loch Raven Community Living & Rehabilitation Center 21218
(3900 Loch Raven Boulevard, 410-605-7000 or 800-463-6295)
Cambridge 21613 (830 Chesapeake Dr., 410-228-6243 or 877-864-9611)
Charlotte Hall 20622 (State Veterans Home, 29431 Charlotte Hall Rd.,
301-884-7102)
Cumberland 21502 (200 Glenn St., 301-724-0061)
Fort Howard 21052 (9600 North Point Rd., 410-477-1800 or 800-351-8387)
Glen Burnie 21061 (808 Landmark Dr., Suite 128, 410-590-4140)
Greenbelt 20770 (7525 Greenway Center Dr., Professional Center Suite
T-4, 301-345-2463)
Hagerstown 21742 (Hub Plaza Bldg, 1101 Opal Ct., 301-665-1462)
Pocomoke 21851 (101 Market St., 410-957-6718 or 866-441-0287)

Regional Office:
Baltimore 21201 (31 Hopkins Plaza Federal Bldg., 1-800-827-1000)

Vet Centers:
Baltimore 21208 (1777 Reisterstown Road, suite 199, 410-764-9400)
Cambridge 21613 (830 Chesapeake Drive, 410-228-6305)
Elkton 21921 (103 Chesapeake Blvd., Suite A, 410-392-4485)
Silver Spring 20910 (1015 Spring St., Suite 101, 301-589-1073)
National Cemeteries:
Annapolis 21401 (800 West St., 410-644-9696/7)
Baltimore 21228 (5501 Frederick Ave., 410-644-9696/7)
Loudon Park 21228 (3445 Frederick Ave., Baltimore, 410-644-9696/7)

MASSACHUSETTS

VA Medical Centers:
Bedford 01730 (200 Springs Rd., 781-687-2000 or 800-422-1617)
Brockton 02301 (940 Belmont St., 508-583-4500)
Jamaica Plain 02130 (150 South Huntington Ave., 617-232-9500)
Leeds 01053-9764 (Northampton VA, 421 North Main St., 413-584-4040 or
   800-893-1522)
West Roxbury 02132 (1400 VFW Parkway, 617-323-7700)

Clinics:
Boston 02114 (251 Causeway St., 617-248-1000)
Dorchester 02121 (895 Blue Hill Ave, 617-822-7146)
Fitchburg 01420 (Burbank Hospital, 275 Nichols Rd., 978-342-9781)
Framingham 01702 (61 Lincoln St., Suite 112, 508-628-0205)
Gloucester 01930 (Addison Gilbert Hospital, 298 Washington St., 978-282-
   0676 ext. 1782)
Greenfield 01301 (143 Munson St., 413-773-8428)
Haverhill 01830 (108 Merrimack St., 978-372-5207)
Hyannis 02601 (233 Stevens St., 508-771-3190)
Lowell 01852 (130 Marshall Rd., 978-671-9000)
Lynn 01904 (225 Boston Rd., Suite 107, 781-595-9818)
Martha's Vineyard 02557 (Hospital Rd., 508-693-0410
Nantucket 02554 (Nantucket Cottage Hospital, 57 Prospect St., 508-825-
   8195)
New Bedford 02740 (175 Elm St., 508-994-0217)
Pittsfield 01201 (73 Eagle St., 413-443-4857)
Quincy 02169 (Quincy Medical Center, 2nd floor, 114 Whitwell St., 617-
   376-2010)
Springfield 01104 (25 Bond St., 413-731-6000)
Worcester 01605 (605 Lincoln St., 508-856-0104)

Regional Office:
Boston 02203-0393 (JFK Federal Building, Room 1265, Government
   Center,
   statewide 1-800-827-1000) (Towns of Fall River & New Bedford,
   counties of Barnstable, Dukes, Nantucket, Bristol, part of Plymouth
   served by
   Providence, R.I., VA Regional Office)

Vet Centers:
Boston 02215 (665 Beacon St., 617-424-0665)
Brockton 02401 (1041-L Pearl St., 508-580-2730)
Hyannis 02601 (474 West Main St., (508-778-0124)
Lowell 01852 (10 George Street, 978-453-1151)
New Bedford 02719 (73 Huttleston Avenue, 508-999-6920)
Springfield 01103 (1985 Main St., Northgate Plaza, 413-737-5167)
Worcester 01605 (691 Grafton St., 508-753-7902)
National Cemetery:

Massachusetts NC 02532 (Connery Ave., Bourne, 508-563-7113/4)

MICHIGAN

VA Medical Centers:

Alpena 49707 (180 North State Avenue, 989-356-8720)
Ann Arbor 48105 (2215 Fuller Rd., 734-769-7100 or 800-361-8387)
Battle Creek 49037 (5500 Armstrong Rd., 269-966-5600 or 888-214-1247)
Clare 48617 (11775 N. Isabella Road, 989-386-3113)
Detroit 48201 (4646 John R. St., 313-576-1000 or 800-511-8056)
Iron Mountain 49801 (325 East H St., 906-774-3300 or 800-215-8262)
Saginaw 48602 (1500 Weiss St., 989-497-2500 or 800-406-5143)

Clinics:

Benton Harbor 49022 (115 Main St., 269-934-9123)
Flint 48532 (G-3267 Beecher Rd., 810-720-2913)
Gaylord 49735 (806 S. Otsego, 989-732-7525)
Grand Rapids 49505 (3019 Coit St., NE, 616-365-9575)
Hancock 49930-1495 (787 Market St., Quincy Center Suite 9, 906-482-7762)
Ironwood 49938 (629 W. Cloverland Dr., Suite 1, 906-932-0032)
Michigan Center 49254 (4328 Page Ave., 517-764-3609)
Kincheloe 49788 (Sault Ste. Marie Clinic: 16523 S. Watertower Dr., Unit 1, 906-495-3030)
Lansing 48910 (2025 S. Washington Ave., 517-267-3925)
Marquette 49855 1414 W. Fair Ave. Suite 285, 906-226-4618)
Manistique (813 East Lakeshore Drive 906-341-3420)
Menominee 49858 (1101 10th Ave., Suite 101, 906-863-1286)
Michigan Center 49254 (4328 Page Ave., 517-764-3609)
Muskegon 49442 (165 E. Apple Ave., Suite 201, 231-725-4105)
Oscoda 48750 (5671 Skeel Ave., Suite 4, 989-747-0026)
Pontiac 48340 (1701 Baldwin Ave., Suite 101, 248-409-0585)
Traverse City 49684 (3271 Racquet Club Dr., 231-932-9720)
Yale 48097 (7470 Brockway Dr., 810-387-3211)

Regional Office:

Detroit 48226 (Patrick V. McNamara Federal Bldg., 477 Michigan Ave., Rm. 1400, 1-800-827-1000)

Vet Centers:

Dearborn 48124-3438 (2881 Monroe St., Suite 100, 313-277-1428)
Detroit 48201 (4161 Cass Ave., 313-831-6509)
Escanaba 49829 (3500 Ludington St. Suite 110, 906-233-0244)
Grand Rapids 49507 (205 Bretib Road, SE Suite 100, 616-285-5795)
Pontiac 48341 (44200 Woodward Avenue, 248-874-1015)
Saginaw 48603 (4048 Bay Rd., 989-321-4650)

National Cemetery:
Fort Custer NC 49012 (15501 Dickman Rd., Augusta, 269-731-4164)
Great Lakes NC 48442 (4200 Belford Rd., Holly, 866-348-8603)

MINNESOTA
VA Medical Centers:
Minneapolis 55417 (One Veterans Dr., 612-725-2000 or 866-414-5058)
St. Cloud 56303 (4801 Veterans Dr., 320-252-1670 or 800-247-1739

Clinics:
Bemidji 56601 (705 5th St., 218-755-6360)
Brainerd 56401 (722 NW 7th St., 218-855-1115)
Fergus Falls 56537 (Veterans Home, 1821 North Park St., 218-739-1400)
Hibbing 55746 (1101 East 37th St., Suite 220, 218-263-9698)
Maplewood 55109 (2785 White Bear Ave., Suite 210, 651-290-3040)
Montevideo 56265 (1025 North 13th St., 320-269-2222)
Rochester 55902 (1617 Skyline Dr., 507-252-0885)
St. James 56081 (1101 Moultin and Parsons Dr., 507-375-3391)

Regional Office:
St. Paul 55111 (Bishop Henry Whipple Federal Bldg., 1 Federal Dr., Fort
    Snelling 1-800-827-1000)
    (Counties of Becker, Beltrami, Clay, Clearwater, Kittson, Lake of the
    Woods,
Mahnomen, Marshall, Norman, Otter Tail, Pennington, Polk, Red Lake,
    Roseau, Wilkin served by Fargo, N.D., VA Regional Office)

Vet Centers:
Brooklyn Park 55445 (701 78th Avenue N, Suite 400, 763-503-2220
Duluth 55802 (405 E. Superior St., 218-722-8654)
St. Paul 55112 (550 County Road D, Suite 10 New Brighton 651-
644-4022

National Cemetery:
Fort Snelling NC 55450-1199 (7601 34th Ave. So., Minneapolis, 612-726-
    1127)

MISSISSIPPI
Medical Centers:
Biloxi 39531 (400 Veterans Ave., 228-523-5000 or 800-296-8872)
Jackson 39216 (1500 E. Woodrow Wilson Dr., 601-362-4471 or 800-949-
    1009, in-state)

Clinics:
Byhalia 38611 (12 East Brunswick St., 662-838-2163)
Columbus 39702 (824 Alabama St., 662-244-0391)

Greenville 38703 (1502 S Colorado St., 662-332-9872)
Hattiesburg 39401 (231 Methodist Blvd., 601-296-3530)
Houlka 38850 (106 Walker St., 662-568-3316)
Kosciusko 39090 (332 Hwy 12W, 662-289-1800)
Meadville 39653 (595 Main Street East, 601-384-3650)
Meridian 39301 (13th St., 601-482-7154)
Natchez 39120 (46 Sgt Prentiss Dr., Ste 16, 601-442-7141)
Smithville 38870 (63420 Highway 25 N., 662-651-4637)

Regional Office:
Jackson 39216 (1600 E. Woodrow Wilson Ave., statewide 1-800-827-1000)

Vet Centers:
Biloxi 39531 (288 Veterans Ave., 228-388-9938)
Jackson 39216 (1755 Lelia Dr., Suite 104, 601-965-5727)

National Cemeteries:
Biloxi NC 39535-4968 (P.O. Box 4968, 400 Veterans Ave., 228-388-6668)
Corinth NC 38834 (1551 Horton St., 901-386-8311)
Natchez NC 39120 (41 Cemetery Rd., 601-445-4981)

MISSOURI
VA Medical Centers:
Columbia 65201-5297 (800 Hospital Dr., 573-814-6000)
Kansas City 64128 (4801 Linwood Blvd., 816-861-4700 or 800-525-1483)
Poplar Bluff 63901 (1500 N. Westwood Blvd., 573-686-4151)
Saint Louis-Jefferson Barracks 63125-4101 (1 Jefferson Barracks Dr., 314-652-4100 or 800-228-5459)
Saint Louis-John Cochran Division 63106 (915 North Grand Blvd., 314-652-4100 or 800-228-5459)

Clinics:
Belton 64012 (17140 Bel-Ray Pl., 816-922-2161)
Branson 65616 (5571 Gretna Rd., 417-243-2300 or 866-951-8387)
Camdenton 65020 (Lake of the Ozarks Clinic, 246 E Highway 54, 573-317-1150)
Cameron 64429 (1111 Euclid Dr., 816-922-2500 ext. 54251)
Cape Girardeau 63701 (2420 Veterans Memorial Dr., 573-339-0909)
Farmington 63640 (1580 W. Columbia St., 573-760-1365)
Ft. Leonard Wood 65473 (126 Missouri Ave., Box 1239, 573-329-8305)
Kirksville 63501 (1108 East Patterson, Suite 9, 660-627-8387)
Jefferson City 65109 (2707 W. Edgewood, 573-635-0233)
Mexico 65265 (Missouri Veterans Home, One Veterans Dr., 573-581-9630)
Mt Vernon 65712 (600 N Main, 417-466-4000 or 800-253-8387)
Nevada 64772 (322 South Prewitt, 417-448-8905)
Paola 66071 (501 S. Hospital Dr, 913-294-4765)

Salem 65560 (Hwy 72 North, 573-729-6626 or 1-888-557-8262)
St. Charles 63304 (7 Jason Ct., 314-286-6988)
St. James 65559-1999 (Missouri Veterans Home, 620 N. Jefferson, St.,
    573 265-0448)
St. Joseph 64506 (1314 North 36th St., Suite A, 1-800-952-8387 ext
    56925)
St. Louis 63136 (10600 Lewis and Clark Blvd, 314-286-6988)
Warrensburg 64093 (1300 Veterans Dr., 816 922-2500 ext. 54281)
Warrensburg 64093 (1300 Veterans Dr., (660) 747-3864
West Plains 65775 (1211 Missouri Ave, 417-257-2454)

Regional Office:
St. Louis 63103 (400 South 18th St., statewide 1-800-827-1000)

Benefits Office:
Kansas City 64128 (4801 Linwood Blvd., 816-922-2660 or 1-800-525-
    1483, x 52660)

Vet Centers:
Kansas City 64111 (301 E. Armour Rd., 816-753-1866)
St. Louis 63103 (2345 Pine St., 314-231-1260)

National Cemeteries:
Jefferson Barracks NC 63125 (2900 Sheridan Rd., St. Louis, 314-845-
    8320)
Jefferson City NC 65101 (1024 E. McCarty St., 314-845-8320)
Springfield NC 65804 (1702 E. Seminole St., 417-881-9499)

MONTANA
VA Medical Centers:
Fort Harrison 59636-1500 (3687 Veterans Drive, P.O. Box 1500, 406-442-
    6410 or 877-468-8387)

Clinics:
Anaconda 59711 (118 East 7th St., 406-563-6090)
Billings 59102 (1775 Spring Creek Ln., 406-373-3500)
Bozeman 59715 (300 N. Wilson, Suite 703G, 406-582-5300)
Cut Bank 59427 (Glacier Community Health, 519 East Main St., 406-873-
    5670)
Glasgow 59230 (630 3nd Ave., South, Suite 107, 406-228-4101)
Glendive 59330 (2000 Montana Ave., 406-377-4755)
Great Falls 59405 (1417-9th St., South, Suite 200/300, 406-791-3200)
Havre 59501, (130 13th Street, Suite 1) (406-265-4304)
Kalispell 59901 (31 Three Mile Dr Ste 102, 406-758-2700)
Lewistown, MT 59457 (629 NE Main St. (Hwy 87) Ste. 1, 406-535-4790)
Miles City 59301 (Clinic / Living Center, 210 S. Winchester, 406-874-5600)

Missoula 59808 (2687 Palmer St., Suite C, 406-829-5400

Regional Office:
Fort Harrison 59636 (3633 Veterans Dr., PO Box 1500, 1-800-827-1000)

Vet Centers:
Billings 59102 (2795 Enterprise Avenue, Suite 1, 406-657-6071)
Missoula 59802 (500 N. Higgins Ave., 406-721-4918)

NEBRASKA

VA Medical Centers:
Grand Island 68803-2196 (2201, No. Broadwell Ave., 308-382-3660/866-580-1810)
Lincoln 68510 (600 South 70th St., 402-489-3802/866-851-6052)
Omaha 68105 (4101 Woolworth Ave., 402-346-8800/800-451-5796)

Clinics:
Alliance 69301 (524 Box Butte Ave., 605-745-2000 ext. 2474)
Bellevue 68113 (2501 Capehart Rd, 402-591-4500)
Grand Island 68803-2196 (2201, No. Broadwell Ave., 308-382-3660/866-580-1810)
Holdrege 68949 (1118 Burlington St., 308-995-3760; 866-580-1810)
Lincoln 68510 (600 South 70th St., 402-489-3802/866-851-6052)
Norfolk 68701 (710 S. 13th St, 402-370-4570)
North Platte 69101 (600 East Francis, Suite 3, 308-532-6906; 866-580-1810)
Rushville/Gordon 69343 (300 E. 8th St., 605-745-2000 ext. 2474,)
Scottsbluff 69361 (1720 E Portal Place, 308-220-3930)
Sidney 69162 (1116 10th Ave., 308-254-5575)

Regional Office:
Lincoln 68516 (5631 S. 48th St., statewide 1-800-827-1000)

Vet Centers:
Lincoln 68510 (3119 O St., 800-228-6838)
Omaha 68131 (2428 Cuming St., 402-346-6735)
National Cemetery:
Fort McPherson NC 69151-1031 (12004 S. Spur 56A, Maxwell, 888-737-2800)

NEVADA

VA Medical Centers:
Las Vegas 89106 (901 Rancho Lane, Mailing Address: P.O. Box 360001, North Las Vegas, NV 89036, 702-636-3000/888-633-7554)
Reno 89502 (1000 Locust Street, 775-786-7200 or 888-838-6256)

Clinics:

Elko 89801 (762 14th St., 775-753-2014)
Ely 89301 (William B. Ririe Hospital, 6 Steptoe Circle, 775-289-3612)
Fallon 89406 (Lahontan Valley Outpatient Clinic: 345 West A St., 775-428-
   6161 or 866-504-0490)
Henderson 89014 (2920 N. Greenvalley Pkwy. Suite 215, 702-636-6363)
Las Vegas 89106 (Center for Homeless Veterans, 916 West Owens Ave.,
   702-636-6380)
Las Vegas 89129 (Northwest Clinic, 2410 Fire Mesa, 702-636-6320)
Las Vegas 89103 (Southwest Clinic, 3880 S. Jones Blvd., 702-636-6390)
Las Vegas 89106 (West Clinic, 630 S. Rancho Rd., 702-636-6355)
Minden 89423 (Carson Valley Clinic, 925 Ironwood Dr., Suite 2102, 888-
   838-6256 x4000)
Pahrump 89048 (2100 E. Calvada Blvd., 775-727-7535)

Regional Office:
Reno 89511 (5460 Reno Corporate Dr., statewide 1-800-827-1000)

Benefits Office:
Las Vegas 89107 (4800 Alpine Pl., Suite 12, 1-800-827-1000)

Vet Centers:
Las Vegas 89146 (1919 So. Jones Blvd., Suite A., 702-251-7873)
Reno 89503 (1155 W. 4th St., Suite 101, 775-323-1294)

NEW HAMPSHIRE
VA Medical Center:
Manchester 03104 (718 Smyth Road, 603-624-4366 or 800-892-8384)

Clinics:
Conway 03818 (7 Greenwood Ave., 603-447-3500 ext. 11)
Littleton 03561 (Littleton Regional Hospital, 600 St. Johnsbury Rd., 603-
   444-9328)
Portsmouth 03803 (Pease International Tradeport 302 Newmarket St., 603-
   624-4366 ext. 5500)
Somersworth 03878 (200 Route 108, 603-624-4366, Ext. 5700)
Tilton 03276 (NH Veterans Home, 139 Winter St., 603-624-4366 ext. 5600)

Regional Office:
Manchester 03101 (Norris Cotton Federal Bldg., 275 Chestnut St., 1-800-
   827-1000)

Vet Center:
Manchester 03104 (103 Liberty St., 603-668-7060/61)
Berlin 03581 (515 Main Street, 603-752-2571)

NEW JERSEY

VA Medical Centers:
East Orange 07018 (385 Tremont Avenue, 973-676-1000)
Lyons 07939 (151 Knollcroft Road, 908-647-0180)

Clinics:
Brick 08724 (970 Rt. 70, 732-206-8900)
Cape May 08204 (1 Monroe Ave., 609-898-8700)
Elizabeth 07206 (654 East Jersey Street, Suite 2A, 908-994-0120)
Fort Monmouth 07703 (Patterson Army Health Clinic, Building 1075,
   Stephenson Ave., 732-532-4500)
Ft. Dix 08640 (Marshall Hall, 8th and Alabama, 609-562-2999)
Hackensack 07601 (385 Prospect Avenue, 201-487-1390)
Jersey City 07302 (115 Christopher Columbus Dr., 201-435-3055/3305)
Morristown 07960 (340 West Hanover Ave., 973-539-9791/9794)
New Brunswick 08901 (317 George Street, 732-729-0646/9555)
Newark 07102 (20 Washington Place, 973-645-1441)
Paterson 07503 (275 Getty Avenue, St. Joseph's Hospital & Medical
   Center, 973-247-1666)
Sewell 08080-2525 (211 County House Road, 856-401-7665)
Trenton 08611-2425 (171 Jersey Street, Bldg. 36, 609-989-2355)
Ventnor 08406 (6601 Ventnor Avenue, Suite 406, 609-823-3122)
Vineland 08360 (Veterans Memorial Home, Northwest Boulevard, 856-692-
   1588)
Vineland 08360 (1051 West Sherman Ave., 856-692-2881)

Regional Office:
Newark 07102 (20 Washington Pl., statewide 1-800-827-1000)
   (Philadelphia,
PA Regional Office serves counties of Atlantic, Burlington, Camden, Cape
   May,
Cumberland, Gloucester, Salem)

Vet Centers:
Bloomfield 07003 (2 Broad St., Suite 703, 973-748-0980)
Ewing 08618 (934 Parkway Ave., 2nd Fl., 609-882-5744)
Lakewood 08701 (1255 Rt. 70, Parkway 70 Plaza, 908-607-6364)
Secaucus 07094 (110 Meadowlands Pkwy., 201-223-7787)
Ventnor 08406 (6601 Ventnor Ave., Suite 105, 609-487-8387)

National Cemeteries:
Beverly 08010 (916 Bridgeboro Rd., 215-504-5610)
Finn's Point 08079 (Box 542, R.F.D. 3, Fort Mott Rd., Salem, 215-504-
   5610)

NEW MEXICO
VA Medical Center:
Albuquerque 87108-5153 (1501 San Pedro Drive, SE, 505-265-1711 or

800-465-8262)

Clinics:
Alamogordo 88310 (1410 Aspen, 575-437-7000)
Artesia 88210-3712 (1700 W. Main St., 575-746-3531)
Durango 81301 (1970 East Third Avenue, Suite 102, (970) 247-2214)
Espanola 87532 (620 Coronado St., Suite B, 505-747-7395)
Farmington 87401-5638 (1001 W. Broadway, Suite C, 505-326-4383)
Gallup 87301 (320 Hwy 564, 505-722-7234)
Las Vegas 87701 (1235 8th St, Las Vegas, 505-425-6788)
Raton 87740-2234 (1275 S. 2nd St., 575-445-2921)
Santa Fe 87505 (2213 Brothers Road, Suite 600, 505-986-8645)
Silver City 88601 (1302 32nd St., 575-538-2921)
Truth or Consequences 87901 (1960 North Date St., 575-894-7662)

Regional Office:
Albuquerque 87102 (Dennis Chavez Federal Bldg., 500 Gold Ave., S.W.,
statewide 1-800-827-1000)

Vet Centers:
Albuquerque 87104 (1600 Mountain Rd. N.W., 505-346-6562)
Farmington 87402 (4251 E. Main, Suite C, 505-327-9684)
Lakewood 08701 (1255 Rt. 70. Parkway 70 Plaza, 908-607-6364)
Las Cruces 88001 (230 S. Water St., 575-523-9826)
Santa Fe 87505 (2209 Brothers Rd., Suite 110, 505-988-6562)

National Cemeteries:
Fort Bayard 88036 (P.O. Box 189, 915-564-0201)
Santa Fe 87501 (501 N. Guadalupe St., 505-988-6400 or toll-free 877-353-
6295)

NEW YORK
Regional Offices:
Buffalo 14202 (Niagara Center, 130 S. Elmwood Ave., 1-800-827-1000)
     (Serves counties not served by New York City VA Regional Office.)
New York City 10014 (245 W. Houston St., statewide 1-800-827-1000)
     (Serves counties of Albany, Bronx, Clinton, Columbia, Delaware,
Dutchess,
Essex, Franklin, Fulton, Greene, Hamilton, Kings, Montgomery, Nassau,
New York,
Orange, Otsego, Putnam, Queens, Rensselaer, Richmond, Rockland,
Saratoga,
Schenectady, Schoharie, Suffolk, Sullivan, Ulster, Warren, Washington,
Westchester.)
Benefits Offices:

Albany 12208 (113 Holland Ave., 1-800-827-1000)
Rochester 14620 (465 Westfall Rd., 1-800-827-1000)
Syracuse 13202 (344 W. Genesee St., 1-800-827-1000)

VA Medical Centers:
Albany 12208 (113 Holland Ave., 518-626-5000)
Batavia 14020 (222 Richmond Ave., 585-297-1000 or 888-798-2302)
Bath 14810 (76 Veterans Ave., 607-664-4000 or 877-845-3247)
Bronx 10468 (130 West Kingsbridge Rd., 718-584-9000 or 800-877-6976)
Brooklyn 11209 (800 Poly Place, 718-836-6600)
Buffalo 14215 (3495 Bailey Ave., 716-834-9200 or 800-532-8387)
Canandaigua 14424 (400 Fort Hill Ave., 585-394-2000)
Castle Point 12511 (Route 9D, 845-831-2000)
Montrose 10548 (2094 Albany Post Rd., Route 9A, 914-737-4400)
New York 10010 (423 East 23rd Street, 212-686-7500)
Northport 11768 (79 Middleville Road, 631-261-4400 or 800-551-3996)
Syracuse 13210 (800 Irving Ave., 315-425-4400 or 800-792-4334)
Domiciliary:
Jamaica 11425 (St. Albans Primary & Extended Care Center, 179-00
   Linden Blvd. & 179 St., 718-526-1000)
Montrose 10548 ((2094 Albany Post Rd., Route 9A, P.O. Box 100, 914-
   737-4400)

Clinics:
Auburn 13021 (17 Lansing St., 315-255-7002)
Bainbridge 13733 (109 North Main St., 607-967-8590)
Binghamton 13901 (Garvin Building, 425 Robinson St., 607-772-9100)
Bronx 10459 (953 Southern Blvd., 718-741-4900)
Brooklyn 11201 (40 Flatbush Ave. Extension, 8th Fl., 718-439-4300)
Carmel 10512 (Provident Savings Bank, 2nd Fl, 1875 Rt 6, 845-228-5291)
Carthage 13619 (3 Bridge St., 315-493-4180)
Catskill 12414 (Columbia Greene Medical Arts Building, Suite A102, 159,
   Jefferson Hgts, 518-943-7515
Clifton Park 12065 (1673 Route 9, 518-383-8506)
Cortland 13045 (1104 Commons Avenue, 607-662-1517)
Dunkirk 14048 (166 East 4th St., 800-310-5001)
Elizabethtown 12932 (PO Box 277 Park St., 518-873-3295)
Elmira 14901 (200 Madison Avenue Suite 2E, 877-845-3247
Fonda 12068 (2623 State Highway 30A, 518-853-1247)
Glens Falls 12801 (84 Broad St., 518-798-6066)
Goshen 10924 (30 Hatfield Lane, Suite 204, 845-294-6927)
Ithaca 14850 (10 Arrowwood Drive, 607-274-4680)
Jamestown 14701 (608 W. 3rd St., 716-338-1511)
Kingston 12401 (63 Hurley Ave., 845-331-8322)
Lackawanna 14218 (OLV Family Care Center, 227 Ridge Rd., 716-822-
   5944)

Lockport 14094 (5883 Snyder Dr., 716-438-3890)

Malone 12953 (183 Park St., 518-481-2545)

Massena 13662 (Memorial Hospital, 1 Hospital Dr., 315-769-4253)

Monticello 12701 (60 Jefferson Street, Unit 3, Lower Parking Lot, 845 791-4936)

New City 10970 (345 N. Main St. upper level, 845-634-8942)

New York 10027 (55 West 125th St., 212-828-5265)

New York 10011 (Opiate Substitution Program, 437 W 16 St., 212-462-4461)

Niagara Falls 14301-2300 (2201 Pine Avenue, 1-800-223-4810)

Olean 14760-2658 (465 North Union St., 716- 373-7709)

Oswego: 13126 (105 County Route 45A Suite 400, 315-343-0925)

Patchogue 11772 (4 Phyllis Drive, 631-475-6610/PC 631-758-4419)

Pine Plains 12567 (2881 Church St., Rt. 199, 518-398-9240)

Plainview 11803 (1425 Old Country Rd., 516-572-8567/PC 516-694-6008)

Plattsburgh 12901 (80 Sharron Ave. 518-561-6247)

Port Jervis 12771 (150 Pike St., 845-856-5396)

Poughkeepsie 12603 (Rt. 55, 488 Freedom Plains Rd., Suite 120, 845-452-5151)

Rochester 14620 (465 Westfall Rd., 585-463-2600)

Rome 13441 (125 Brookley Road, Building 510, 315-334-7100)

Schenectady 12308 (1322 Gerling Street, Sheridan Plaza, 518-346-3334)

Springville 14141 (27 Franklin Street, 716 592-7400)

Staten Island 10314 (1150 South Ave, 3rd Floor – Suite 301, 718-761-2973)

Sunnyside 11104 (41-03 Queens Blvd., 718-741-4800)

Troy 12180 (295 River St., 518-274-7707)

Warsaw 14569 (Wyoming County Community Hospital, 400 North Main St., 585-786-2233)

Wellsville 14895 (3458 Riverside Dr., Route 19, 1-877-845-3247)

Westhampton 11978 (Community Air Base: 150 Old Riverhead Rd., 631-898-0599)

White Plains 10601 (23 South Broadway, 914-421-1951)

Yonkers 10705 (124 New Main St., 914-375-8055)

Regional Offices:

Buffalo 14202 (Niagara Center, 130 S. Elmwood Ave., 1-800-827-1000)
   (Serves counties not served by New York City VA Regional Office.)

New York City 10014 (245 W. Houston St., statewide 1-800-827-1000)
   (Serves counties of Albany, Bronx, Clinton, Columbia, Delaware, Dutchess,

Essex, Franklin, Fulton, Greene, Hamilton, Kings, Montgomery, Nassau, New York,

Orange, Otsego, Putnam, Queens, Rensselaer, Richmond, Rockland, Saratoga,

Schenectady, Schoharie, Suffolk, Sullivan, Ulster, Warren, Washington,

Westchester.)
Benefits Offices:
Albany 12208 (113 Holland Ave., 1-800-827-1000)
Rochester 14620 (465 Westfall Rd., 1-800-827-1000)
Syracuse 13202 (344 W. Genesee St., 1-800-827-1000)

Vet Centers:
Albany 12205 (17 Computer Drive West., 518-626-5130)
Babylon 11702 (116 West Main St., 631-661-3930)
Bronx 10468 (2471 Morris Avenue, 718-367-3500)
Brooklyn 11201 (25 Chapel St., Suite 604, 718-624-2765)
Buffalo 14228 (2372 Sweet Home Road, 716-862-7350)
Middletown 10940 (726 East Main street Suite 203 845-342-9917)
New York 10004 (32 Broadway, Suite 200, 212-742-9591)
New York 10035 (2279 3rd Avenue, 212-426-2200)
Rochester 14620 (1867 Mt. Hope Ave., 585-232-5040)
Staten Island 10301 (150 Richmond Terrace, 718-816-4499)
Syracuse 13210 (716 E. Washington St., 315-478-7127)
White Plains 10601 (300 Hamilton Ave., 1st Fl., 914-682-6250)
Watertown 02601 (210 Court St., 315-782-0217
Woodhaven 11421 (75-10B 91st Ave., 718-296-2871)
Binghamton 13901 (53 Chenango St,. 607-722-2393)
Plainview 11803 (1425 Old Country Rd. 516-572-8455)

National Cemeteries:
Bath 14810 (76 Veterans Ave., San Juan Ave., 607-664-4853/4806)
Calverton 11933-1031 (210 Princeton Blvd., 631-727-5410/5770)
Cypress Hills 11208 (625 Jamaica Ave., Brooklyn, 631-454-4949)
Long Island 11735-1211 (2040 Wellwood Ave., Farmingdale, 631-454-
   4949)
Saratoga 12871-1721 (200 Duell Rd., Schuylerville, 518-581-9128)
Woodlawn 14901 (1825 Davis St., Elmira, 607-732-5411)

NORTH CAROLINA
VA Medical Centers:
Asheville 28805 (1100 Tunnel Road, 828-298-7911 or 800-932-6408)
Durham 27705 (508 Fulton St., 919-286-0411)
Fayetteville 28301 (2300 Ramsey St., 910-488-2120 or 800-771-6106)
Salisbury 28144 (1601 Brenner Avenue, 704-638-9000 or 800-469-8262)

Clinics:
Charlotte 28213 (8601 University East Drive, 704-597-3500)
Durham 27705 (1824 Hillandale Road, 919-383-6107)
Franklin 28734 (647 Wayah St., 828-369-1781)
Greenville 27858 (800 Moye Blvd., 252-830-2149)
Hamlet 28345 (100 Jefferson St., 910-582-3536)

Hickory 28601 (1170 Fairgrove Church Rd., 828-431-5600)
Jacksonville 28540 (1021 Hargett St., 910-219-1339)
Morehead City 28557 (5420 Highway 70, 252-240-2349)
Raleigh 27610 (3305 Sungate Blvd., 919-212-0129)
Wilmington 28401 (1606 Physicians Dr., Suite 104, 910-362-8811)
Winston-Salem 27103 (190 Kimel Park Dr., 336-768-3296)

Regional Office:
Winston-Salem 27155 (Federal Bldg., 251 N. Main St., statewide 1-800-
   827-1000,
nationwide Loan Guaranty Certificate of Eligibility Center 1-888-244-6711)

Vet Centers:
Charlotte 282602 (2114 Ben Craig Drive, Suite 300, 704-549-8025223 S.
Brevard St., Suite 103, 704-333-6107)
Fayetteville 28311 (4140 Ramsey St., Suite 110, 910-488-6252)
Greensboro 27406 (2009 S. Elm-Eugene St., 336-333-5366)
Greenville 2783458 (1021 WH Smith Blvd., Suite 100, 150 Arlington Blvd.,
Suite B, 252-355-7920)
Raleigh 27604 (1649 Old Louisburg Rd., 919-856-4616)

National Cemeteries:
New Bern 28560 (1711 National Ave., 252-637-2912)
Raleigh 27610-3335 (501 Rock Quarry Rd., 252-637-2912)
Salisbury 28144 (501 Statesville Blvd., 704-636-2661/4621)
Wilmington 28403 (2011 Market St., 252-637-2912)

NORTH DAKOTA
VA Medical Center:
Fargo 58102 (2101 Elm Street, 701-232-3241 or 800-410-9723)

Clinics:
Bismarck 58503 (2700 State Street, 701-221-9152)
Dickinson 58601 (33 9th Street, 701-483-6017)
Grafton 58237 (Developmental Center Health Service Building, West Sixth
   Street, 701-352-4059)
Jamestown 58401 (419 Fifth Street NE, 701-952-4787)
Minot 58705 (10 Missile Avenue, 701-727-9800)
Williston 58801 (3 Fourth Street East, Suite 104, 701-577-9838)

Regional Office:
Fargo 58102 (2101 Elm St., statewide 1-800-827-1000)

Vet Centers:
Bismarck 58501 (1684 Capital Way, 701-224-9751)
Fargo 58103 (3310 Fiechtner Dr., Suite 100, 701-237-0942)

Minot 58701 (1400 20th Avenue SW, Suite 22041 3rd St. N.W., 701-852-0177)

OHIO
VA Medical Centers:
Brecksville 44141 (10000 Brecksville Rd., 440-526-3030)
Chillicothe 45601 (17273 State Route 104, 740-773-1141 or 800-358-8262)
Cincinnati 45220 (3200 Vine Street, 513-861-3100 or 888-267-78730)
Cleveland 44106 (10701 East Blvd., 216-791-3800)
Columbus 43209 (420 N. James Road, 614-257-5200 or 888-615-9448)
Dayton 45428 (4100 W. 3rd Street, 937-268-6511 or 800-368-8262)

Clinics:
Akron 44319 (55 W. Waterloo 330-724-7715)
Ashtabula 44004 (1230 Lake Avenue, 866-463-0912)
Athens 45701 (510 West Union Street 740-593-7314)
Cambridge 43727 (2146 Southgate Pkwy., 740-432-1963)
Canton 44702 (733 Market Avenue South, 330-489-4600)
Cincinnati 45245 (4355 Ferguson Drive, Suite 270, 513-943-3680)
Cleveland 44113 (4242 Loraine Ave., 216-939-0699)
East Liverpool 43920 (15655 St Rt. 170, 330-386-4303)
Grove City 43123 (1955 Ohio Avenue, 614-257-5800)
Hamilton 45011 (1755-C South Erie Highway, (513) 870-9444)
Lancaster 43130 (1550, Sheridan Drive Colonnade Medical Bldg., 740-653-6145)
Lima 45804 (1303 Bellefontaine Ave., 419-222-5788)
Lorain 44052 (205 West 20th Street, 440-244-3833)
Mansfield 44906 (1456 Park Avenue West, 419-529-4602)
Marietta 45750 (418 Colegate Drive, 740-568-0412)
Marion 43302 (1203 Delaware Avenue, Corporate Center #2, 740-223-8089)
Middletown: 45042 (675 North University Boulevard, 513-423-8387)
New Philadelphia 44663 (1260 Monroe Ave., Suite 1A, New 330) 602-5339)
Newark 43055 (1912 Tamarck Rd., 740-788-8329)
Painesville 44077 (7 West Jackson Street, 440-357-6740)
Portsmouth 45622 (820 Gallia St., 740-353-3236)
Ravenna 44266 (6751 N. Chestnut St., 330-296-3641)
Sandusky 44870 (3416 Columbus Avenue, 419-625-7350)
Springfield 45505 (512 South Burnett Road, 937-328-3385
St. Clairsville 43950 (107 Plaza Dr., 740-695-9321)
Toledo 43614 (3333 Glendale Avenue, 419-259-2000)
Warren 44485 (1400 Tod Ave. (NW), 330-392-0311)
Youngstown 44505 (2031 Belmont Avenue, 330-740-9200)
Zanesville 43701 (2800 Maple Avenue, 740-453-7725)

Regional Office:
Cleveland 44199 (Anthony J. Celebrezze Fed. Bldg., 1240 E. 9th St.,
1-800-827-1000)
Benefits Offices:
Cincinnati 45202 (36 E. Seventh St., Suite 210, 1-800-827-1000)
Columbus 43215 (420 James Rd., 1-800-827-1000)

Vet Centers:
Cincinnati 45203 (801-B W. 8th Street., Suite 126, 513-763-3500)
Cleveland Heights 44118 (2022 Lee Rd., 216-932-8471)
Columbus 43215 (30 Spruce St., 614-257-5550)
Dayton 454028 (One Elizabeth Place111 W 1st St., Suite 101, 937-461-
9150)
Parma 44129 (5700 Pearl Rd., Suite 102, 440-845-5023)
Toledo 43614 (1565 S. Byrne Rd., Suite 104, 419-213-7533)

National Cemeteries:
Dayton 45428-1088 (4100 W. Third St., 937-262-2115)
Ohio Western Reserve 44270 (10175 Rawiga Rd., Rittman, 330-335-3069)

OKLAHOMA
VA Medical Centers:
Muskogee 74401 (1011 Honor Heights Drive, 918-577-3000 or 888-397-
8387)
Oklahoma City 73118 (1024 N.W. 47th Street, Suite B, 405-456-5184)

Clinics:
Altus 73521 (201 S. Park Lane. 580-482-9020)
Ardmore: 73401 (2002 12th Ave. NW, Suite E, 580-226-4580)
Enid 73701 (915 E. Garriott, Suite G., 580-242-5100)
Fort Sill 73503 (4303 Pittman and Thomas Bldg. 580-585-5600)
Jay (1569 North Main Street 918-253-1900 or 888-424-8387)
Konawa 74849 (527 W 3rd St. P.O. Box 358, 580-925-3286)
Hartshorne 74547 (1429 Pennsylvania Ave., 888-878-1598)
Stillwater 74074 (1815 West 6th Street, 405-743-7300)
Tulsa 74145 (9322 East 41st St., 918-628-2500)
Ponca City/Blackwell 74631 (1009 W. Ferguson Ave, 580-363-0052)
Vinita 74301 (269 S. 7th St. 918-713-5400)
Wichita Falls 76301 (1800 7th Street, 940-723-2373)
Oklahoma City Satellite Clinic "North May Clinic" 73120 (2915 Pine Ridge
Road, 405-752-6500)

Regional Office:
Muskogee 74401 (Federal Bldg., 125 S. Main St., Compensation &
Pension: 1-800-827-1000, Education National Call Center: 1-888-442-
4551, National Direct Deposit: 1-877-838-2778)

Benefits Office:
Oklahoma City 73102 (Federal Campus, 301 NW 6th St., Suite 113, 1-800-827-1000)

Vet Centers:
Lawton 73501 (1016 SW, C Avenue Suite B, 580-585-5885)
Oklahoma City 73118 (1024 N.W. 47th, 405-270-5184)
Tulsa 74112 (1408 S. Harvard, 918-748-5105)

National Cemeteries:
Fort Gibson 74434 (1423 Cemetery Rd., 918-478-2334)
Fort Sill 73538 (2648 NE Jake Dunn Rd., 580-492-3200)

OREGON
VA Medical Centers:
Portland 97239 (3710 SW U.S. Veterans Hospital Rd., 503-220-8262 or outside Portland area 800-949-1004)
Roseburg 97470 (913 NW Garden Valley Blvd., 541-440-1000 or 800-549-8387)

Clinics:
Bandon 97411 (1010 1st Street, SE, Suite 100, 541-347-4736)
Bend 97701 (2115 NE Wyatt Ct., Suite 201, 503-220-8262 or outside Portland area 800-949-1004)
Brookings 97415 (555 Fifth Street, 541-412-1152)
Burns-Hines Outreach Clinic 97720 (271 N. Egan Burns, OR 541-573-8869)
Eugene 97404 (100 River Ave., 541-607-0897)
Hillsboro 97006 (1925 Amber Glen Parkway Ste #300, 503-906-5000 or outside Portland area 800-949-1004)
Klamath Falls 97601 (2819 Dahlia St., 541-273-6206)
La Grande, OR 97850 (202 12th St., 541-963-0627)
Portland 97220 (10535 NE Glisan St., Gateway Medical Bldg., 2nd Fl., 503-220-8262, or outside Portland area 800-949-1004
Salem 97301 (1660 Oak Street SE, 503-220-8262 or outside Portland area 800-949-1004)
Salem 97301 (1660 Oak Street SE Ste #100, 503-220-8262, or outside Portland area 800-949-1004)
Warrenton 97146 (91400 Rilea Neacoxie St., Building 7315, 503-220-8262, or outside Portland area 800-949-1004)
White City 97503 Rehab & Clinics (8495 Crater Lake Hwy., 541-826-2111)

Regional Office:
Portland 97204 (Edith Green/Wendell Wyatt Federal Building, 1220 S.W. Third Ave., 1-800-827-1000)

Vet Centers:

Eugene 97403 (1255 Pearl St., 541-465-6918)
Grants Pass 97526 (211 S.E. 10th St., 541-479-6912)
Portland 97220 (8383 N.E. Sandy Blvd., Suite 110, 503-273-5370)
Salem 97301 (12645 Portland road, NE., Suite 250

National Cemeteries:
Eagle Point 97524 (2763 Riley Rd., 541-826-2511)
Roseburg 97470 (1770 Harvard Blvd, 541-826-2511)
Willamette 97266-6937 (11800 S.E. Mt. Scott Blvd., Portland, 503-273-5250)

PENNSYLVANIA
VA Medical Centers:
Altoona 16602 (2907 Pleasant Valley Boulevard, 814-943-8164)
Butler 16001 (325 New Castle Road, 724-287-4781 or 800-362-8262)
Coatesville 19320 (1400 Black Horse Hill Road, 610-384-7711)
Erie 16504 (135 East 38 Street, 814-868-8661 or 800-274-8387)
Lebanon 17042 (1700 South Lincoln Avenue, 717-272-6621 or 800-409-8771)
Philadelphia 19104 (University and Woodland Avenues, 800-949-1001 or 215-823-5800)
Pittsburgh 15260 (Delafield Road, 866-482-7488 or 412-688-6000)
Pittsburgh 15206 (Highland Drive Division: 7180 Highland Drive, 412-365-4900 or 1-866-4VAPITT)
Pittsburgh 15240 (University Drive Division: University Drive, 1-866-482-7488)
Wilkes-Barre 18711 (1111 East End Blvd., 570-824-3521 or 877-928-2621)

Clinics:
Allentown 18103 (3110 Hamilton Boulevard, 610-776-4304 or 866-249-6472)
Bangor 18013 (701 Slate Belt Boulevard, 610-599-0127)
Bradford 16701 (23 Kennedy Street, Suite 101, 814-368-3019)
Berwick 18603 (301 W. Third Street, 570-759-0351)
Camp Hill 17011 (25 N. 32nd Street, 717-730-9782)
DuBois 15801 (190 West Park Avenue, Suite 8, 814-375-6817)
Ellwood City 16117 (Ellwood City Hospital, Medical Arts Building, Suite 201, 304 Evans Drive 724-285-2203)
Foxburg 16036 (ACV Medical Center, 855 Route 58, Suite 1, 724-659-5601)
Frackville 17931 (10 East Spruce St., 570-874-4289)
Franklin 16323 (Venango County Clinic, Pennwood Center, 464 Allegheny Boulevard, 866-962-3260
Greensburg 15601 (Hempfield Plaza, Route 30, 724-837-5200)
Hermitage 16148 (295 N. Kerrwood Dr., Suite 110, 724-346-1569)
Horsham 19044 (433 Caredean Dr., 215-823-6050)

Johnstown 15904 (1425 Scalp Ave., Suite 29, 814-266-8696)
Kittanning 16201 (Armstrong Memorial Hospital 1 Nolte Dr., 724-543-8711)
Lancaster 17605 (1861 Charter Lane, Green Field Corporate Center, Suite 118, 717-290-6900)
Meadville 16335 (18955 Park Ave. Plaza, 866-962-3210)
Monaca 15061 (90 Wagner Rd., 724-216-0326)
New Castle 16101 (Jameson Hospital, 1000, S. Mercer Street, 724-285-2203)
Northampton Clinic & Rehab Ctr (701 Slate Belt Boulevard Bangor 610-597-0127)
Philadelphia 19106 (214 North 4th Street, 215-923-2600)
Pottsville 17901 (Good Samaritan Medical Mall, 700 Schuylkill Manor Road, Suite 6, 570-621-4115)
Reading 19601 (St. Joseph's Community Center, 145 N. 6th St., 610-208-4717)
Sayre 18840 (1537 Elmira St., 570-888-6803)
Schuylkill 17972 (6 South Greenview Rd., 570-621-4115)
Spring City 19475 (11 Independence Drive 610-948-0981)
Springfield 19064 (Crozer Keystone Healthplex, 194 W. Sproul, Road, Suite 105, 610-543-3246)
State College 16801 (3048 Enterprise Drive, 814-867-5415)
Tobyhanna 18466 (Tobyhanna Army Depot Building 220, 570-615-8341)
Uniontown 15401 (404 W. Main St., 724-439-4990)
Warren 16365 (3 Farm Colony Dr., 866-682-3250)
Washington 15301 (100 Ridge Avenue, 724-250-7790)
Wilkes-Barre 18711 (1111 East End Boulevard, 570-924-3521)
Williamsport 17701 (1705 Warren Avenue, Werner Building – 3rd Floor, Suite 304, 570-322-4791)
York 17402 (1797 Third Avenue, 717-854-2481 or 717-854-2322)
Regional Offices:
Philadelphia 19101 (Regional Office and Insurance Center, P.O. Box 8079, 5000 Wissahickon Ave., 1-800-827-1000; Serves counties of Adams, Berks,
Bradford, Bucks, Cameron, Carbon, Centre, Chester, Clinton, Columbia, Dauphin,
Delaware, Franklin, Juniata, Lackawanna, Lancaster, Lebanon, Lehigh, Luzerne,
Lycoming, Mifflin, Monroe, Montgomery, Montour, Northampton, Northumberland,
Perry, Philadelphia, Pike, Potter, Schuylkill, Snyder, Sullivan, Susquehanna, Tioga,
Union, Wayne, Wyoming, York.)
Pittsburgh 15222 (1000 Liberty Ave., statewide 1-800-827-1000. Serves remaining
counties of Pennsylvania.)

Benefits Office:
Wilkes-Barre 18702 (1123 East End Blvd., Bldg. 35, Suite 11, 1-800-827-1000)

Vet Centers:
Erie 16501 (1000 State St., Suite 1&2, 814-453-7955)
Dubois 15801 (100 Meadow Lane, Suite 8, 814-372-2095)
Harrisburg 17102 (1500 N. 2nd St., Suite 2, 717-782-3954)
McKeesport 15131 (2001 Lincoln Way, 412-678-7704)
Norristown 19401 (314 E. Johnson Highway, Suite 201)
Philadelphia 19107 (801 Arch St., Suite 102, 215-627-0238)
Philadelphia 19120 (101 E. Olney Ave., 215-924-4670)
Pittsburgh 15205 (2500 Baldwick Rd., Suite 15, 412-920-1765)
Scranton 18505 (1002 Pittston Ave., 570-344-2676)
Williamsport 17701 (49 E. Fourth Street, Suite 104, 570-327-5281)

National Cemeteries:
Indiantown Gap 17003-9618 (R.R. 2, P.O. Box 484, Indiantown Gap Rd., Annville, 717-865-5254/5)
Cemetery of the Alleghenies 15017 (1158 Morgan Rd., Bridgeville, 724-746-4363)
Philadelphia 19138 (Haines St. & Limekiln Pike, 215-504-5610)
Washington Crossing 18940 (830 Highland Rd., Newtown, 215-504-5610)

PHILIPPINES
Clinics:
Pasay City 1300 (2201 Roxas Blvd., 011-632-833-4566)

Regional Office:
Manila 0930 (1131 Roxas Blvd., 011-632-528-6300, International Mailing Address: PSC 501, DPO AP 96515-1100)

PUERTO RICO
Medical Center:
San Juan 00921-3201 (10 Casia Street, 787-641-7582 or 800-449-8729)

Clinics:
Arecibo 00612 (Victor Rojas II / Zona Industrial Carr. 129, 787-816-1818)
Guayama 00784 (FISA Bldg 1st Floor, Paseo Del Pueblo, km 0.3, lote no 6, 787-866-8766)
Mayagüez 00680-1507 (Avenida Hostos #345, 787-265-8805)
Ponce 00716-2001(Paseo Del Veterano #1010, 787-12-3030)
Regional Office:
San Juan 00918-1703 (150 Carlos Chardon Ave., Suite 300. Send mail

to Suite 232. Serving all Puerto Rico and the Virgin Islands, 1-800-827-1000)

Benefits Offices:
Mayaguez 00680-1507 (Ave. Hostos 345, Carretera 2, Frente al Centro Medico, 1-800-827-1000)
Ponce 00731 (10 Paseo del Veterano, 1-800-827-1000)
Arecibo 00612 (Gonzalo Marin 50, 1-800-827-1000)

Vet Centers:
Arecibo 00612-4702 (52 Gonzalo Marin St., 787-879-4510/4581)
Ponce 00731 (35 Mayo St., 787-841-3260)
San Juan 00921 (Condominio Med. Ctr. Plaza, Suite LC8A11, La Riviera, 787-749-4409)
National Cemetery:
Puerto Rico 00961 (Ave. Cementerio Nacional 50, Barrio Hato Tejas, Bayamon, 787-798-8400)

RHODE ISLAND
VA Medical Center:
Providence 02908 (830 Chalkstone Avenue, 401-273-7100 or 866-590-2976)

Clinic:
Middletown 02842 (One Corporate Place, 401-847-6239)

Regional Office:
Providence 02903 (380 Westminster St.; statewide, 1-800-827-1000)

Vet Center:
Warwick 02889 (2038 Warwick Ave., 401-739-0167)

SOUTH CAROLINA
Regional Office:
Columbia 29209 (6437 Garners Ferry Rd., statewide 1-800-827-1000)

VA Medical Centers:
Charleston 29401 (109 Bee Street, 843-577-5011 or 888-878-6884)
Columbia 29209 (6439 Garners Ferry Road, 803-776-4000)

Clinics:
Aiken 29803 (951 Millbrook Ave., 803-643-9016)
Anderson 29621 (1702 E. Greenville Street, 864-224-5450)
Beaufort 29902 (Pickney Road, 843-770-0444)
Florence 29505 (1822 Sally Hill Farms Blvd. 843-292-8383)
Greenville 29605 (3510 Augusta Rd., 864-299-1600)

Myrtle Beach 29577 (3381 Phillis Blvd. , 843-477-0177)
North Charleston 29406 (9237 University Blvd, 843-789-6400)
Orangeburg 29118 (1767 Villagepark Drive, 803-533-1335)
Rock Hill 29730 (205 Piedmont Blvd, 803-366-4848)
Spartanburg 29303 (279 North Grove Medical Park Drive, 864-582-7025)
Sumter 29150 (407 North Salem Avenue, 803-938-9901)
Nursing Home:
Walterboro 29488 (2461 Sidneys Road, Veterans Victory House, 843-538-3000)
Nursing Home:
Walterboro 29488 (2461 Sidneys Road, Veterans Victory House, 843-538-3000)

Regional Office:
Columbia 29209 (6437 Garners Ferry Rd 1-800-827-1000)

Vet Centers:
Charleston 29406 (5603-A Rivers Avenue, 843-789-7000)
Columbia 29201 (11710-A Richland Street, 803-765-9944)
Greenville 29601 (14 Lavinia Ave., 864-271-2711)
North Charleston 29406 (5603-A Rivers Ave., 843-747-8387)

National Cemeteries:
Beaufort 29902-3947 (1601 Boundary St., 843-524-3925)
Florence 29501 (803 E. National Cemetery Rd., 843-669-8783)
Fort Jackson 29229 (4170 Percival Rd., Columbia, 803-699-2246)

SOUTH DAKOTA
VA Medical Centers:
Fort Meade 57741 (113 Comanche Road, 605-347-2511 or 800-743-1070)
Hot Springs 57747 (500 North 5th Street, 605-745-2000 or 800-764-5370)
Sioux Falls 57105 (2501 W. 22nd Street, 605-336-3230 or 800-316-8387)

Clinics:
Aberdeen 57201 (917 29th St. SE, 605-622-2640)
Eagle Butte 57625 (15 Main Street, 605-9672644)
McLaughlin, SD 57642 (302A Sale Barn Rd., 605-823-4574)
Mission 57555 (153 Main Street, 605-856-2295)
Pierre 57501 (1601 North Harrison, Suite 6, 605-945-1710)
Pine Ridge (605-718-1905)
Rapid City 57701 (3525 5th Street, 605-718-1095)
Wagner 57380 (400 W. Hwy. 46-50, 605-384-2340)
Watertown 57201 (917 29th St. SE, 605-884-2420)
Winner 57580 (1436 E. 10th St., 605-842-2443)

Regional Office:

Sioux Falls 57105 (2501 W. 22nd St., statewide 1-800-827-1000)
Vet Centers:
Martin 57551 (105 East Hwy 18, 605-685-1300)
Rapid City 57701 (621 6th St., Suite 101, 605-348-0077)
Sioux Falls 57104 (601 S. Cliff Ave., Suite C, 605-330-4552)

National Cemeteries:
Black Hills 57785 (20901 Pleasant Valley Dr., Sturgis, 605-347-3830)
Fort Meade 57785 (P.O. Box 640, Old Stone Rd., Sturgis, 605-347-3830)
Hot Springs 57747 (500 N 5th St., 605-347-3830)

TENNESSEE
VA Medical Centers:
Memphis 38104 (1030 Jefferson Avenue, 901-523-8990 or 800-636-8262)
Mountain Home 37684 (Corner of Lamont and Sydney Streets, P.O. Box
    4000, 423-926-1171 or 877-573-3529)
Murfreesboro 37129 (3400 Lebanon Pike, 615-867-6000 or 800-876-7093)
Nashville 37212 (1310 24th Avenue South, 615-327-4751 or 800-228-
    4973)

Clinics:
Tullahoma 37389 (225 First Street, 931-454-6134)
Chattanooga 37411 (150 Debra Rd., Suite 5200, Bldg. 6200, 423-893-
    6500)
Clarksville 37043 (1832 memorial St, 931-645-3552
Cookeville 38501 (851 S. Willow Avenue, Suite 108, 931-284-4060)
Covington 38127 (N. Memphis, 3461 Austin Peay Highway, 901-261-4500)
Dover 37204 (1021 Spring Street, 931-232-5329)
McMinnville (1014 S. Chancery Street, 931-474-7700)
Meharry (1818 Albion Street, Nashville, TN 615-329-4818)
Memphis 38116 (1056 East Raines Rd., 901-271-4900)
Morristown 37813 (925 E. Morris Blvd., 423-586-9100)
Nashville (Women's Clinic, 1919 Charlotte Ave 615-873-8000)
Vine Hill 37204 (601 Benton Ave, Nashville, 615-292-9770)
Knoxville 37923 (9031 Cross Park Drive, 865-545-4592)
Savannah 38372 (765-A Florence Rd, 731-925-2300)

Regional Office:
Nashville 37203 (110 9th Ave., South, statewide 1-800-827-1000)

Vet Centers:
Chattanooga 37411 (951 Eastgate Loop Rd., Bldg. 5700, Suite 300, 423-
    855-6570)
Johnson City 37604 (1615A W. Market St., 423-928-8387)
Knoxville 37914 (2817 E. Magnolia Ave., 865-545-4680)
Memphis 38104 (1835 Union, Suite 100, 901-544-0173)

Nashville 37217 (Airpark Bus. Cen. 1, Suite A-5, 1420 Donelson Pike, 615-366-1220)

National Cemeteries:
Chattanooga 37404 (1200 Bailey Ave., 423-855-6590)
Knoxville 37917 (939 Tyson St., N.W., 423-855-6590)
Memphis 38122 (3568 Townes Ave., 901-386-8311)
Mountain Home 37684 (P.O. Box 8, VAMC, Bldg. 117, 423-979-3535)
Nashville 37115-4619 (1420 Gallatin Rd. S., Madison, 615-860-0086)

TEXAS
VA Medical Centers:
Amarillo 79106 (6010 Amarillo Boulevard West 806-355-9703 or 800-687-8262)
Big Spring 79720 (300 Veterans Blvd., 432-263-7361 or 800-472-1365)
Bonham 75418 (1201 E. 9th Street, 903-583-2111 or (800) 924-8387)
Dallas 75216 (4500 South Lancaster Road, 214-742-8387 or 800-849-3597)
El Paso 79930 (5001 North Piedras Street, 915-564-6100 or 800-672-3782)
Harlingen 78550 (South Texas VA Health Care Center, 2106 Treasure Hills Blvd,, 956-366-4500)
Houston 77030 (2002 Holcombe Blvd., 713-791-1414 or 800-553-2278)
Kerrville 78028 (3600 Memorial Blvd, 830-896-2020)
San Antonio 78229 (7700 Merton Minter Blvd., 877-469-5300 or 888-686-6350
Temple 78613 (1901 Veterans Memorial Drive, 254-778-4811 or 800-423-2111)
Waco 76711 (4800 Memorial Drive, 254-752-6581 or 800-423-2111)

Clinics:
Abilene 79602 (4225 Woods Place, 432-263-7361)
Austin 78741 (2901 Montopolis Drive, 512-389-1010)
Beaumont 77707 (3420 Veterans Circle, 409-981-8550 or 1-800-833-7734)
Beeville 78102 (302 S. Hillside Dr., 361-358-9912)
Bridgeport 76426 (812 Woodrow Wilson Ray Cir., 940-683-2297)
Brownwood 76801 (2600 Memorial Park Drive, 325-641-0568)
Cedar Park 78613 (701 Whitestone Boulevard, 512-260-1368)
Childress 79201 (1001 Hwy 83 North, 940-937-3636
Cedar Park 78613 (701 East Whitestone Boulevard. 512-260-1368)
Bryan/College Station 77845 (1651 Rock Prairie Road, Suite 100, 979-680-0361))
Conroe 77304 (800 Riverwood Ct., Ste. 100, 936-522-4000 800-553-2278, ext. 1949)
Corpus Christi 78405 (5283 Old Brownsville Road, 361-806-5600)
Denton 76205 (2223 Colorado Blvd., 800-310-5001)

Fort Worth 76104 (300 W., Rosedale Street, 817-335-2202 or 800-443-9672)

Fort Worth 76107 (855 Montgomery Street, 817-735-2228)

Fort Stockton 79735 (501 N. Main, 432-263-7361)

Galveston 77550 (3828 Ave N, 409-761-3200 or 800-553-2278, ext. 12600)

Granbury 76049 (2006 Fall Creek Hwy., 817-326-3440)

Greenville 75407 (4006 Wellington Rd., Ste. 100, 903-450-4788)

Harlingen 78550 (2106 Treasure Hills Blvd, 956-366-4500)

La Grange 78945 (890 E. Travis Street 979-968-5878)

Laredo 78041 (6551 Star Court, 956-523-7850, refills: 1-800-209-7377)

Longview 75601 (1205 E. Marshal Ave., 903-247-8262 or 800-957-8262)

Lubbock 79412 (6104 Avenue Q South Drive, 806-472-3400)

Lufkin 75904 (12206 North John Redditt Drive, 936-671-4300 or 1-800-209-3120)

McAllen 78503 (2101 S. Colonel Rowe Blvd, 956-618-7100 or 866-622-5536)

New Braunfels 78130 (189 E. Austin, Suite 106, 830-629-3614)

Odessa 79762 (4241 N. Tanglewood, Suite 201, 432-263-7361)

Palestine 75801 (2000 So. Loop 256, Suite 124, 903-723-9006)

Paris 75460 (635 Stone Ave., 903-785-9900)

San Antonio 78240 (Frank M, Tejeda OPC, 5788 Eckhert Road, 210-699-2100)

San Antonio Dental Clinic 78299 (8410 Data Point, 210-949-8900)

San Angelo 76905 (2018 Pulliam, 432-263-7361)

San Antonio 78226 (1831 S. General McMullen, 210-434-1400)

San Antonio Greenway 78217 (2455 NE Loop 410, Ste. 100, 210- 599-6000)

San Antonio Northern Hills 78217 (14100 Nacogdoches, Ste. 116, 210-653-8989)

San Antonio Pecan Valley 78222 (4243 E Southcross, Ste. 205, 210-304-3500)

Sherman 75090 (3811 US 75N., 903-487-0477)

Stamford 79553 (Box 911, Hwy 6 East, 432-263-7361)

Stratford 79084 (1220 Purnell, P.O. Box 1107, 806-396-2852)

Tyler 75701 (3414 Golden Rd, 903-593-3050)

Victoria 77901 (1502 E. Airline Dr.Suite 40, 361-582-7700 or 800-209-7377)

Wichita Falls 76301 (1800 7th St., 940-723-2373)

Regional Offices:

Houston 77030 (6900 Almeda Rd., statewide, 713-383-1999 or 1-800-827-1000. Serves counties of Angelina, Aransas, Atacosa, Austin, Bandera, Bee, Bexar, Blanco, Brazoria, Brewster, Brooks, Caldwell, Calhoun, Cameron, Chambers, Colorado, Comal, Crockett, DeWitt, Dimitt, Duval, Edwards, Fort Bend, Frio, Galveston, Gillespie, Goliad, Gonzales, Grimes, Guadeloupe, Hardin, Harris, Hays, Hidalgo, Houston, Jackson,

Jasper, Jefferson, Jim Hogg, Jim Wells, Karnes, Kendall, Kennedy, Kerr, Kimble, Kinney, Kleberg, LaSalle, Lavaca, Liberty, Live Oak, McCulloch, McMullen, Mason, Matagorda, Maverlck, Medina, Menard, Montgomery, Nacogdoches, Newton, Nueces, Orange, Pecos, Polk, Real, Refugio, Sabine, San Augustine, San Jacinto, San Patricio, Schleicher, Shelby, Starr, Sutton, Terrell, Trinity, Tyler, Uvalde, Val Verde, Victoria, Walker, Waller, Washington, Webb, Wharton, Willacy, Wilson, Zapata, Zavala) Waco 76799 (One Veterans Plaza, 701 Clay Ave; statewide, 1-800-827-1000; serves the rest of the state. In Bowie County, the City of Texarkana is served by Little Rock, AR, VA Regional Office, 1-800-827-1000.)

Benefits Offices:
Abilene 79602 (Taylor County Plaza Bldg., Suite 103, 400 Oak St., 1-800-827-1000)
Amarillo 79106 (6010 Amarillo Blvd. W., 1-800-827-1000)
Austin 78741 (2901 Montopolis Dr., Room 108, 1-800-827-1000)
Corpus Christi 78405 (4646 Corona Dr., Suite 150, 1-800-827-1000)
Dallas 75216 (4500 S. Lancaster Rd., 1-800-827-1000)
El Paso 79930 (5001 Piedras Dr., 1-800-827-1000)
Ft. Worth 76104-4856 (300 W. Rosedale St., 1-800-827-1000)
Lubbock 79410 (6104 Ave. Q S Drive, Rm. 132, 1-800-827-1000)
McAllen 78503 (109 Toronto Ave., 1-800-827-1000)
San Antonio 78240 (5788 Eckert Rd., 1-800-827-1000)
Temple 76504 (1901 Veterans Memorial Dr., Room 5G38 [BRB], 1-800-827-1000)
Tyler 75701 (1700 SSE Loop 323, Suite 310, 1-800-827-1000)

Vet Centers:
Amarillo 79109 (3414 Olsen Blvd., Suite E., 806-354-9779)
Austin 78741 (2015 S I.H. 35, Suite 101, 512-416-1314)
Corpus Christi 78411 (4646 Corona, Suite 250, 361-854-9961)
Dallas 75231 (10501 N. Central Expressway, Suite 213, 214-361-5896)
El Paso 79925 (1155 Westmoreland, Suite 121, 915-772-0013)
Fort Worth 76104 (1305 W. Magnolia, Suite B, 817-921-9095)
Killeen Heights 76548 (302 Millers Crossing, Suite #4, 254-953-7100)
Harris County 77014 (14300 Cornerstone Village Dr., #110, 713-578-4002)
Houston 77098 (2990 Richmond Ave., Suite 325, 713-523-0884)
Houston 77024 (701 N. Post Oak Rd., Suite 102, 713-682-2288)
Laredo 78041 (6020 McPherson Rd., 1A, 956-723-4680)
Lubbock 79410 (3208 34th St., 806-792-9782)
McAllen 78504 (801 W Nolana Loop, Suite 140, 956-631-2147)
Midland 79705 (2817 W. Loop 250N Suite E, 432-697-8222)
San Antonio 78212 (231 W. Cypress St., Suite 100, 210-472-4025)

National Cemeteries:
Dallas-Fort Worth 75211 (2000 Mountain Creek Parkway, 214-467-3374)

Fort Bliss 79906 (Box 6342, 5200 Fred Wilson Rd., 915-564-0201)
Fort Sam Houston 78209 (1520 Harry Wurzbach Rd., San Antonio, 210-820-3891/3894)
Houston 77038 (10410 Veterans Memorial Dr., 281-447-8686)
Kerrville 78028 (VAMC, 3600 Memorial Blvd., 210-820-3891/3894)
San Antonio 78202 (517 Paso Hondo St., 210-820-3891/3894)

UTAH
VA Medical Center:
Salt Lake City 84148 (500 Foothill Drive, 801-582-1565 or 800-613-4012)

Clinics:
Fountain Green 84632 (300 W. 300 S., 435-623-3129)
Nephi 84648 (48 W. 1500 N., 435-623-3129)
Ogden 84403 (982 Chambers Street, 801-479-4105)
Orem 84057 (740 W. 800 N., Suite 440, 801-235-0953)
Roosevelt 84066 (210 W. 300 N. (75-3), 435-725-2082)
St. George 84770 (1067 East Tabernacle, Suite 7, 435-634-7608 Ext. 6000)

Regional Office:
Salt Lake City 84158 (P.O. Box 581900, 550 Foothill Dr., statewide 1-800-827-1000)

Vet Centers:
Provo 84604 (1807 No. 1120 West, 801-377-1117)
Salt Lake City 84106 (1354 East 3300 South, 801-584-1294)

VERMONT
VA Medical Center:
White River Junction 05009 (215 North Main Street, 802-295-9363 or 866-687-8387)

Clinics:
Bennington 05201 (186 North Street, 802-447-6913)
Colchester 05446 (162 Hegeman Ave., Unit 100, 802-655-1356)
Littleton, NH 03561 (685 Meadow St., Suite 4, 603-444-1323)
Rutland 05701 (215 Stratton Road, 802-770-6713)

Regional Office:
White River Junction 05009 (215 N. Main St., 802-296-5177 or 1-800-827-1000 from within Vermont)

Vet Centers:
Gorham, NH 03581 (515 Main St., 603-752-2571)
South Burlington 05403 (359 Dorset St., 802-862-1806)
White River Junction 05001 (222 Holiday Inn Dr., #2 Gilman Office

Complex, 802-295-2908 or 1-800-649-6603)

VIRGINIA

VA Medical Centers:
Hampton 23667 (100 Emancipation Drive, 757-722-9961)
Richmond 23249 (1201 Broad Rock Boulevard, 804-675-5000 or 800-784-8381)
Salem 24153 (1970 Roanoke Boulevard, 540-982-2463 or 888-982-2463)

Clinics:
Alexandria 22301 (6940 South Kings Highway Suite #208, 703-313-0694)
Charlottesville 22911 (650 Peter Jefferson Pkwy., 434-293-3890)
Danville 24540 (705 Piney Forrest Rd., 434-710-4210)
Fredericksburg 22401 (1960 Jefferson Davis Hwy., Suite 100, 540-370-4468)
Harrisonburg 22801 (847 Cantrell Avenue, Suite 100, 540-442-1773)
Hillsville 24343 (702 Pine St., 276-779-4220)
Lynchburg 24501 (1600 Lakeside Drive, 434-316-5000)
Martinsville 24112 (315 Hospital Way, Ste. 101, 276-632-5929)
Stephens City 22655 (106 Hyde Court, 540-869-0600)
Saltville 23470 (308 W. Main St., 276-496-4433)
Tazewell 24651 (123 Ben Bolt Ave., 276-988-2526)
Virginia Beach 23462 (244 Clearfield Ave., 757-726-6070)

Regional Office:
Roanoke 24011 (210 Franklin Rd., S.W., statewide 1-800-827-1000)

Vet Centers:
Alexandria 22310 (86940 South Kings Highway, Suite 204, 703-360-8633)
Norfolk 23504 (1711 Church Street, suite 1&2, 757-623-7584)
Richmond 23230 (4902 Fitzhugh Ave., 804-353-8958)
Roanoke 24016 (350 Albemarle Ave., SW, 540-342-9726)
Virginia Beach 23452 (324 South Port Circle, suite 102)

National Cemeteries:
Alexandria 22314 (1450 Wilkes St., 703-221-2183/2184)
Balls Bluff 22075 (Rte. 7, Leesburg, 540-825-0027)
City Point 23860 (10th Ave. & Davis St., Hopewell, 804-795-2031)
Cold Harbor 23111 (6038 Cold Harbor Rd., Mechanicsville, 804-795-2031)
Culpeper 22701 (305 U.S. Ave., 540-825-0027)
Danville 24541 (721 Lee St., 704-636-2661)
Fort Harrison 23231 (8620 Varina Rd., Richmond, 804-795-2031)
Glendale 23231 (8301 Willis Church Rd., Richmond, 804-795-2031)
Hampton 23667 (Cemetery Rd. at Marshall Ave., 757-723-7104)
Hampton 23669 (VAMC, Emancipation Dr., 757-723-7104)
Quantico 22172 (P.O. Box 10, 18424 Joplin Rd. (Rte. 619), Triangle 703-

221-2183/2184)
Richmond 23231 (1701 Williamsburg Rd., 804-795-2031)
Seven Pines 23150 (400 E. Williamsburg Rd., Sandston, 804-795 2031/2278)
Staunton, 24401 (901 Richmond Ave., 540-825-0027)
Winchester 22601 (401 National Ave., 540-825-0027)

VIRGIN ISLANDS
Clinics:
St. Croix 00850-4701 (Village Mall, 16, Box 10553 RR02, Kingshill, 340-778-5553)
St. Croix (TMedical Foundation Bldg., Suite 1010, 50 Estate Thomas), Suite 304 & 310,
St. Thomas Medical Foundation, 340- 774-6674

Benefits:
Served by San Juan, Puerto Rico, VA Regional Office, 1-800-827-1000

Vet Centers:
St. Croix 00850 (Box 12, R.R. 02, Village Mall, 113, RR2 Box 10556, Kingshill, 340-778-5553)
St. Thomas 00802 (9800 Buchaneer Mall, Suite 8, 340-774-6674)

WASHINGTON
VA Medical Centers:
Seattle 98108 (1660 S. Columbian Way, 800-329-8387 or 206-762-1010)
Spokane 99205 (4815 N. Assembly Street, 509-434-7000 or 800-325-7940)
Tacoma 98493 (9600 Veterans Dr., 253-582-8440 or 800-329-8387)
Vancouver 98661 (1601 E. 4th Plain Blvd, 360-696-4061 or 800-949-1004)
Walla Walla 99362 (77 Wainwright Drive, 509-525-5200 or 888-687-8863)

Clinics:
Bellevue 98005 (13033 Bel-Red Road, Suite 210, 425-214-1055)
Bremerton 98312 (925 Adele Avenue, 360-782-0129)
Federal Way 98003 (34617 11th Place South, 253-336-4142)
Mobile Medical Unit (Aberdeen, Shelton and Morton, 253-583-1162)
Port Angeles 98362 (1005 Georgianna St., 360-565-9330)
Richland 99352 (Richland Federal Bldg., 825 Jadwin Ave., Ste. 250, 509-946-1020)
Seattle 98125 (12360 Lake City Way NE, Suite 200, 206-384-4382)
Sedro Woolley 98284 (2031-C Hospital Drive, Cedar Grove Building B, 360-856-4700)
Wenatchee 98801 (2530 Chester-Kimm Road, 509-663-7615)
Yakima 98902 (717 Fruitvale Blvd., 509-966-0199)
Yakima Mental Health Clinic 98902 (2119 W. Lincoln Ave, 509-457-2736

Regional Office:
Seattle 98174 (Fed. Bldg., 915 2nd Ave., statewide 1-800-827-1000)
Benefits Offices:
Fort Lewis 98433 (Waller Hall Rm. 700, P.O. Box 331153, 253-967-7106)
Bremerton 98337 (W. Sound Pre-Separation Center, 262 Burwell St., 360-782-9900)˙

Vet Centers:
Bellingham 98226 (3800 Byron Ave., Suite 124, 360-733-9226)
Everett 98201 (3311 Wetmore Ave, Everett, WA, 425-252-9701)
Seattle 98121 (2030 9th Ave., Suite 210, 206-553-2706)
Spokane 99206 (100 N. Mullan Rd., Suite 102, 509-444-8387)
Tacoma 98409 (4916 Center St., Suite E, 253-565-7038)
Yakima 98902 (2119 W. Lincoln Ave., 509-457-2736)
National Cemetery:
Tahoma 98042-4868 (18600 S.E. 240th St., Kent, 425-413-9614)

WEST VIRGINIA

VA Medical Centers:
Beckley 25801 (200 Veterans Avenue, 304-255-2121 or 877-902-5142)
Clarksburg 26301 (One Medical Center Drive, 304-623-3461 or 800-733-0512)
Huntington 25704 (1540 Spring Valley Drive, 304-429-6741 or 800-827-8244)
Martinsburg 25405 (510 Butler Avenue, 304-263-0811 or 800-817-3807)

Clinics:
Charleston 25304 (104 Alex Ln., 304-926-6001)
Franklin 26807 (314 Pine Street, 304-358-2355)
Logan 25601 (513 Dingess St., 304-752-8355
Morgantown 26501 (40 Commerce Drive, Suite 101, 304-292-7535)
Parkersburg 260101 (2311 Ohio Avenue, Suite A, 304-422-5114)
Parsons 26287 (206 Spruce Street, 304-478-2219)
Petersburg 26847 (Grant Memorial Hospital, P. O. Box 1019, 304-257-5817)
Sutton 26602 (93 Skidmore Lane, 304-765-3480)
Williamson 25661 (75 W 4th Ave, 304-235-2187)

Regional Office:
Huntington 25701 (640 Fourth Ave., statewide 1-800-827-1000; counties of Brooke, Hancock, Marshall, Ohio, served by Pittsburgh, Pa., VA Regional Office)

Vet Centers:
Beckley 25801 (1000 Johnstown Rd. 304-252-8220)

Charleston 25302 (521 Central Ave., 304-343-3825)
Huntington 25701 (3135 16th St. Rd., Suite 11, 304-523-8387)
Martinsburg 25401 (900 Winchester Ave., 304-263-6776)
Morgantown 26508 (1083 Greenbag Rd., 304-291-4303)
Princeton 24740 (905 Mercer St., 304-425-5653)
Wheeling 26003 (1058 Bethleham Rd., 304-232-0587)

National Cemeteries:
Grafton 26354 (431 Walnut St., 304-265-2044)
West Virginia 26354 (Rt. 2, Box 127, Grafton, 304-265-2044)

WISCONSIN
VA Medical Centers:
Madison 53705 (2500 Overlook Terrace, 608-256-1901)
Milwaukee 53295 (5000 West National Avenue, 888-469-6614 or 414-384-2000)
Tomah 54660 (500 E. Veterans Street, 608-372-3971 or 800-872-8662)

Clinics:
Appleton 54914 (10 Tri-Park Way, 920-831-0070)
Baraboo 53913 (626 14th Street, 608-356-9318)
Beaver Dam 53916 (215 Corporate Drive, 920-356-9415)
Chippewa Falls 54729 (2501 & 2503 County Hwy I, 715-720-3780)
Cleveland 53015 (1205 North Avenue, 920-693-5600)
Green Bay 54303 (141 Siegler Street, 920-497-3126)
Hayward 54843 (15748 County Road B, 715-934-5454)
Janesville 53545 (111 N. Main Street, 608-758-9300)
Kenosha 53140 (800 55th Street, 262-653-9286)
La Crosse 54601 (2600 State Road, Phone: 608-784-3886)
Loyal 54446 (141 N. Main Street, 715-255-9799)
Rhinelander 54501 (639 West Kemp Street, 715-362-4080)
Rice Lake 54843 (2700A College Drive, 715-236-3355)
Superior 54880 (3520 Tower Avenue, 715-392-9711)
Union Grove 53182 (21425 Spring Street, 262-878-7000)
Wausau 54401 (515 South 32nd Avenue, 715-842-2834)
Wisconsin Rapids 54494 (710 East Grand Ave., PO Box 26, 715-424-3844)

Regional Office:
Milwaukee 53214 (5400 W. National Ave., statewide 1-800-827-1000)

Vet Centers:
Madison 53703 (706 Williamson St., 608-264-5342)
Green Bay 54304 (1600 E. Ashland Avenue, 920-435-5650)
Milwaukee 53218 (5401 N. 76th St., 414-536-1301)

National Cemetery:
Wood 53295-4000 (5000 W. National Ave., Bldg. 1301, Milwaukee,

414-382-5300)

WYOMING

VA Medical Centers:
Cheyenne 82001 (2360 E. Pershing Blvd., 307-778-7550 or 888-483-9127)
Sheridan (1898 Fort Road, 307-672-3473 or 866-822-6714)

Clinics:
Afton Outreach Clinic 83110 (125 S. Washington 307-886-5266)
Casper 82601 (4140 S. Poplar St., 307-235-4143 or 1-866-338-5168)
Gillette 82718 (604 Express Drive, 307-685-0676 or 1-866-612-1887)
Newcastle 57555 (1124 Washington Blvd., 605-745-2000 ext. 2474)
Powell 82435 (777 Avenue H, 307-754-7257 or 1-888-284-9308)
Riverton 82501 (2300 Rose Lane, 307-857-1211 or 1-866-338-2609)
Rock Springs 82901 (1401 Gateway Blvd., 307-362-6641 or 866-381-2830)

Benefits Office:
Cheyenne 82001 (2360 E. Pershing Blvd., statewide 1-800-827-1000)

Vet Centers: Casper 82601 (1030 North Poplar, Suite B, 307-261-5355)
Cheyenne 82001 (3219 East Pershing Blvd., 307-778-7370)

Index

FEDERAL BENEFITS FOR VETERANS, DEPENDENTS AND SURVIVORS 2010
Publication Order Form

Order Processing Code
3557

Toll Free: 866 512–1800
Phone: 202 512–1800
Fax: 202 512–2104

Mail: US Government Printing Office
P.O. Box 979050
St. Louis, MO 63197–9000

Easy Secure Internet: bookstore.gpo.gov

❏ **YES!** please send me_____copies of *Federal Benefits for Veterans, Dependents and Survivors 2010*. S/N 051–000–00238–5, single copies only. $5.00 per single copy.

❏ **YES!** please send me_____*"Beneficios Federales para los Veteranos, sus Dependientes y Sobrevivientes" 2010*. S/N 051–000–00239–3, single copies only. $5.00 per single copy.

The total cost of my order is $_____. Price includes regular postage and handling and price is subject to change. International customer please add 40%. Price subject to change without notice.

Personal name   (Please type or print)

Company name

Street address

City, State, Zip code

Daytime phone including area code

Charge your order, It's easy!   **VISA**   MasterCard   DISCOVER NOVUS   AMERICAN EXPRESS

❏ **Check payable to *Superintendent of Documents***

❏ **SOD Deposit Account** ⬚⬚⬚⬚⬚⬚⬚ — ⬚

❏ **VISA** ❏ **MasterCard** ❏ **Discover/NOVUS** ❏ **American Express**

⬚⬚⬚⬚⬚⬚⬚⬚⬚⬚⬚⬚⬚⬚⬚⬚⬚   Thank you for your order!

⬚⬚⬚⬚ (expiration date)   **GPO**

Authorizing signature

03/10

**Federal Benefits for Veterans,
Dependents and Survivors
VA Pamphlet 80-10-01
P94663**

U.S. Department of Veterans Affairs
Washington, DC 20420

OFFICIAL BUSINESS

ISBN 978-0-16-085220-6

9 780160 852206

9 0 0 0 0